The Monk: Adaptations for the Stage

The Monk: Adaptations for the Stage

Edited with an Introduction by

Jasmine A. Ramón

Whitlock Publishing
Alfred, NY

The Monk: Adaptations for the Stage

First Whitlock Publishing edition 2015

Whitlock Publishing
P.O. Box 472
Alfred, NY 14802

ISBN 13: 978-1-943115-01-3

Acknowledgements

Special thanks to Dr. Allen Grove for his help with layout and revisions. Also, credit to Anaïs Jeanine Ramón for her work on the cover design.

Table of Contents

Introduction

> *"The back of the cavern falls to pieces, and discovers the* BLEEDING NUN, *in a blue ethereal flame, invoking a blessing upon them—she slowly ascends, still blessing them—they form a tableau, and the curtain descends."*
>
> —Conclusion to *Raymond and Agnes*

> "Raymond presents Agnes to his Father, who joins their hands; and the piece concludes with A FINALE SPANISH FANDANGO."
>
> —Conclusion to *Airs, Glees and Chorusses*

True to late eighteenth-century melodrama, the sensational excesses of these finales give the contemporary reader a glimpse into the largely forgotten world of Romantic period theatre. Matthew Gregory Lewis' *The Monk*, popular for its sexual and religious deviance, was adapted for the stage less than a year after its publication in 1796. With its reputation as 'the most Gothic of eighteenth century Gothic romances,' *The Monk* has been transformed for theatre and film numerous times over the centuries (Watt 71). Two of the plays in this volume—*Raymond and Agnes* and *Airs, Glees, and Chorusses*—rip from the pages of *The Monk* the love story of Raymond and Agnes as they are persecuted by robbers. James Boaden's *Aurelio and Miranda* reinvents *The Monk*'s scandalous affair between Ambrosio and Matilda. The passion, repression, and romance of the couples are conveyed through dance, pantomime, chorus, and dialogue, and the Bleeding Nun makes her appearance in two of the plays to bestow her blessing and help the central couples achieve their 'happily ever after.'

The Life of Lewis

Matthew Gregory Lewis was born on July 9, 1775, to Matthew Lewis and Frances Maria Sewell. He did not like either of his names, so often he went by M. G. Lewis, and after the success of his novel, "Monk" Lewis. His parents did not have the best marriage; despite his father's wealth, Lewis began writing in order to support his mother, who had left him and his three other siblings for a music master when he was six. Lewis maintained a relationship with his mother even as he continued his education the way his father wanted. He earned his degree from Christ Church College, Oxford. By the end of his education, he had become a diplomat, and with his father's help got a position with the British Embassy in The Hague. He published *The Monk* anonymously, but the praise he received was enough for him to add his name and title, Member of Parliament (M.P.), to the title page of the following edition. Even though Lewis's father had enough political power to obtain a seat on Parliament for his son, Lewis was more interested in writing than government and politics. He only lasted as an M.P. for a single term. When his father died in 1812, Lewis' playwright career was replaced by the responsibility of overseeing his father's estate. After his first trip to his father's Jamaican plantations, Lewis expressed concern over the slaves' welfare. He visited in 1815 and then again in 1817, and decided to pursue reforms for the slaves' working conditions. His will stated that those reforms be maintained even if he died, and a journal of his travels was published posthumously in 1834, entitled *Journal of a West India Proprietor, Kept During a Residence in the Island of Jamaica*. During a return trip from Jamaica in 1818, Lewis died from complications with yellow fever and was buried at sea, although "in a final Gothic irony, the weights attached to the coffin came off, and the coffin rose to the surface and drifted out of sight toward Jamaica" (Hamm 162).

Lewis as "Monk"

Inspired by Ann Radcliffe's *The Mysteries of Udolpho,* Lewis completed *The Monk* in three volumes by March 1796, and the novel's success quickly followed its publication. Whereas critics attacked the novel's immorality, readers were allured by the temptation, repression, and romance that were entwined with the work's Spanish and Catholic setting. The novel's improprieties, in fact, were clearly appealing to the public. Within two years of its publication, *The Monk* had gone through four editions.

There was, however, much opposition to the scandalous content of the novel. Lewis's rapid rise to fame was undercut by moralists and religious people who criticized his portrayal of the Catholic Church, his depiction of the Devil, his critique of the Bible, and the sexual excesses of gender-changing Rosario. The threat of prosecution and disappointment from his father encouraged Lewis to make changes to the fourth edition. He allowed his sister, Maria, to edit the novel and remove the parts she did not see as fit or proper for publication. After her changes, *The Monk* was published without the offensive language and sexually explicit scenes. Nevertheless, the original version remained popular and in circulation, confirming that Lewis had created what would become an important addition to Gothic fiction. In one particular fourth edition of *The Monk* that resurfaced in the last decade, the original eighteenth-century owner had hand written and bound the 'naughty bits' back into the novel, proving a certain amount of dedication to every last lurid detail.

***The Monk*'s Impact on Other Writers**

During Lewis' time, Europe was generally moving to separate Church and state after a long tug of war between Protestantism and Catholicism during which many were prosecuted and killed. However, Britain was slow to realize this separation. Even critic Samuel Taylor Coleridge, who admired Lewis for his imagination and other works, pointed out the novel's inappropriateness. The particularly blasphemous scene in *The Monk,* in which Antonia reads from a Bible edited by her mother, caught the attention of religious figures such as Reverend Thomas James Mathias who created a satiric piece to criticize it. His critique of the novel asks, "Is this a time to poison the waters of our land in their springs and fountains? Are we to add incitement to incitement, and corruption to corruption, till there neither is, nor can be, a return to virtuous action and to regulated life?" (Mathias 293). The Bible scene is so controversial because it suggests that the holy book itself is improper; Antonia's mother removes passages she thought would corrupt the mind of her innocent daughter. Mathias fails to see the inappropriateness of the Bible, but he does go on to point out other authors who were prosecuted for printing obscene books. Lewis indirectly addresses criticism such as this within *The Monk* when Raymond talks to Theodore about writing: "An author, whether good or bad, or between both, is an animal whom everybody is privileged to attack: for though all are not able to write books, all conceive themselves able to judge them" (Lewis). Lewis' novels after *The Monk* were never quite as popular or controversial as his first work. Lewis mastered the Gothic genre with his play *The Castle Spectre,* which was first performed in December 1797 at Drury Lane Theatre, and then in Covent Garden after a quarrel with Richard Brinsley Sheridan. The play, like *The Monk*, involved disguise, revelation of familial ties, and ghostly specters. Despite trying to branch out from the Gothic genre, it was clear that that was where he belonged. Today he is mostly known for *The Monk,* and is credited with influencing Lord Byron, Sir Walter Scott, and possibly Percy Bysshe Shelley and John William Polidori.

The Rise of the Gothic

Horace Walpole is often credited with having begun the Gothic novel genre with the writing of *The Castle of Otranto* in 1764. Centered on a new kind of romance that blends the conventions of the modern novel with the ancient romance, the Gothic reached the height of its popularity in the 19th century, particularly with the works of Mary Shelley (*Frankenstein*), Bram Stoker (*Dracula*), and Edgar Allan Poe ("The Raven," "Tell-Tale Heart"). Gothic fiction is distinguished by its settings in crumbling, haunted castles or churches filled with abandoned rooms and hidden passages. Often these settings are rendered even more terrifying by being visited during the darkest part of the night or the most horrendous storm. Other conventions of Gothic novels are mysterious family secrets, a damsel in distress and, of course, her dashing hero. And perhaps most important for a work like Lewis' is the inclusion of the supernatural. The Bleeding Nun and other ghostly specters and demons lurk in both the shadows and plain sight. We can see many of the conventions of the genre when Raymond describes Agnes's drawing of the ghostly nun:

> I took up some of the drawings, and cast my eyes over them. One of the subjects struck me with its singularity. It represented the great hall of the castle of Lindenberg. A door conducting to a narrow staircase stood half open. In the foreground appeared a group of figures, placed in the most grotesque attitudes; terror was expressed upon every countenance. Here was one upon his knees, with his eyes cast up to heaven, and praying most devoutly; there, another was creeping away upon all fours. Some hid their faces in their cloaks or the laps of their companions; some had concealed themselves beneath a table, on which the remnants of a feast were visible; while others, with gaping mouths and eyes wide-stretched, pointed to a figure supposed to have created this disturbance. It represented a female of more than human stature, clothed in the habit of some religious order. Her face was veiled; on her arm hung a chaplet of beads; her dress was in several places stained with the blood which trickled from a wound upon her bosom. In one hand she held a lamp, in the other, a large knife, and she seemed advancing towards the iron gates of the hall. (Lewis 99-100)

This description of the Bleeding Nun is a true representation of the Gothic, equally vivid and terrifying. Yet despite Agnes's attention to detail in her painting, when Raymond asks her whether or not she believes in the Bleeding Nun, she replies, "How can you ask such a question? No, no…" (Lewis 102). Characters such as Raymond and Agnes put their faith in reason and are unwilling to acknowledge the existence of supernatural creatures. Lewis, however, has not created a reasonable world. He makes *The Monk* interesting by suggestioning that those who put faith in the supernatural often have a better understanding of reality than those who don't. Only when Raymond and Agnes come to recognize and deal with the existence of the Bleeding Nun can they be reunited. Yet Lewis' harshest condemnation is not directed at either the rational or the superstitious, but those who are in charge of corrupt and hypocritical religious institutions. The monk Ambrosio and the Prioress meet equally gruesome deaths, and the novel as a whole presents strong anti-Catholic sentiments. The authors of the adaptations in this collection didn't dare make the same kinds of assertions, and the questions of faith and superstition that got Lewis in trouble barely make an appearance on the stage.

Lovers on the Stage

Charles Farley's 1797 *Airs, Glees, And Chorusses In A New Grand Ballet Pantomime Of Action, Called Raymond And Agnes; Or The Castle Of Lindenbergh* and Henry William Grosette's 1810 *Raymond and Agnes; or the Bleeding Nun of Lindenberg* work equally to acknowledge the supernatural, but the characters do not hold the same beliefs towards it. The Bleeding Nun appears as an agent to reunite Raymond and Agnes, but Farley's work concludes with the blessing of Raymond's father, a more realistic ending. *Raymond and Agnes,* on the other hand, completely buys into the supernatural with a conclusion involving a tableau and the ascending Bleeding Nun. However, the plays present little connection between the supernatural and reality in sharp contrast to the original novel. In *Raymond and Agnes,* the plot builds when Agnes is hidden in the robber's cave from Raymond by the bandits. Typical of romance, men must battle for possession of the heroine:

> *Raymond attacks Robert, who falls wounded; and as he rises, and aims a blow at Raymond, Marguerette snatches a pistol from his belt, and shoots him—Agnes rises—Theodore darts furiously on Claude, and overcomes him—Jaques is shot by Agnes with a pistol dropped by Claude.—Raymond and Agnes meet—they embrace, and kneel.*

This final fight is more fitting of the conventions of a romantic play than a Gothic one. All of the sexual transgressions and physical suffering we find in the novel are gone as Raymond and Agnes assume conventional hero and heroine roles. The playwrights have created much less controversial plots than *The Monk*.

The most shocking and unconventional relationship in *The Monk*, the sexual affair of Ambrosio and Matilda within monastery walls, becomes a sentimental and relatively chaste relationship in James Boaden's 1799 theater adaptation, *Aurelio and Miranda*. The play begins with Aurelio as the father figure of Eugenio, much like the novel with Ambrosio and Rosario. The gender switching remains in the adaptation as well, and Eugenio unveils as Miranda in a manner similar to the novel. The play places much more emphasis on Aurelio's struggle with rejecting Miranda's advances because he is a religious figure. Miranda is less of a temptress and more of a proper lady, a heroic one even, since she goes to save Agnes and reunite her with Raymond. In fact, Aurelio doesn't truly yield to her until she is revealed to be a lady of status, the sister of Captain Christoval, a far cry from the demon Matilda turns out to be in Lewis' work. Aurelio too, originally an orphan, realizes he was born to nobility, thus making it acceptable for him to step away from the Church in order to claim his title and take a wife. Ultimately, instead of continuing down the path of darkness as they do in the novel, the infamous couple not only chooses redemption and reformation, but their nobility allows them to have a socially acceptable union.

Ambrosio and Matilda cross many lines of eighteenth-century propriety. Matilda, with her transformation from the young boy Rosario, to the temptress Matilda, and ultimately to the Devil himself, introduced carnality and the lure of evil into a church setting. Her ability to unleash Ambrosio's sexual desire and make him unholy called into question the relationship between religious duty and sexual passion. In the infamous "beauteous orb" scene of *The Monk*, religion is ultimately no match for lust and desire. Ambrosio, the most Godlike of men in the eyes of Madrid, proves mere man as he faces the breast of Matilda:

> She had torn open her habit, and her bosom was half exposed. The weapon's point rested upon her left breast: And Oh! that was such a breast! The Moonbeams darting full upon it enabled the Monk to observe its dazzling whiteness. His eye dwelt with insatiable avidity upon the beauteous Orb. (Lewis 46)

Ambrosio is driven mad by the sight of her breast, and in the novel this moment quickly leads to couple's sexual union. The play has no such carnal scenes. Nevertheless, the novel was remarkably popular, while the play had only a brief run. Clearly English society desired its entertainment to include dark, unconventional and perhaps even depraved love affairs.

Late Eighteenth- and Early Nineteenth-Century English Theater

Though the theater was popular, contemporary scholars find few impressive plays from the late eighteenth and early nineteenth centuries. A slow, discernible change came to the stage in the last decade of the eighteenth century. Productions took on a rather mimetic nature, extracting plots from the novels of the time and adapting them for the stage. The novel was the most popular form of literature in the late eighteenth century, and it was not uncommon for stage adaptations of popular novels to appear in theaters mere weeks after publication.

While the plays may not be a high point for dramatic literature, the theaters themselves developed significantly. The Theatre-Royal Covent-Garden was built in 1663 by order of Thomas Killigrew. Just three years earlier, the monarchy had been restored with the crowning of King Charles II, and one of his first acts was to reopen the theaters that the Puritans had closed down in 1642. Killegrew and Sir William Davenant were granted approval by Charles II to build two theaters solely for plays. At the time, Killigrew's venue was known as the Theatre Royal in Bridges Street. This theater underwent two makeovers before Lewis' time. After the theater burned down in 1672, it was rebuilt and reopned in 1674 as the Theatre Royal in Drury Lane.

In 1732, John Rich opened the Theatre Royal, Covent Garden. The Licensing Act of 1737 wiped out many competing theaters by censoring all the plays without expressed permission of Lord Chamberlain (Donohue 11). By the 1790s, Drury Lane and Convent-Garden dominated the theater world. Covent-Garden was renovated and expanded in 1792, and it was here that Mr. Farley's ballet of *Raymond and Agnes* was performed in 1797. At nearby Drury Lane, Richard Brinsely Sheridan tore down the theater to build a larger facility that opened in 1794. This new venue was where James Boaden's *Aurelio and Miranda* ran for six nights in 1799. These changes to the theaters increased capacity and raised profits by better providing for London's growing population. The name 'Theatre Royal' was popular at the time; Drury Lane was one of three theaters with the name (The other two being the Theatre Royal at Haymarket and Theatre Royal at Covent Garden). Sharing the name added further friction to the competition between theaters. Even then, there was still more competition with theaters scattered around London: Sadler's Wells, the Royal Circus, Pantheon and Lyceum, to name a few. However, Drury Lane was most popular, with the most up-to-date technology of the time and the best painted scenes (Donohue 19).

Class and the Theater

Over time, the playhouse became a mark of the middle class, a place to make a statement and build reputation. It was clear not all the seats in the theater were equal; there was a range of exclusivity that was more easily transcended, if only for a performance, than the class system that existed outside the theater doors. Of course there were rules as to where women were allowed and more indirect commentary on what it meant to sit in certain seats. By the end of the century, theaters had increasingly become places for fashionable, social spectacle, not just entertainment. Tourism and social habits also affected programming, and the different seasons of theater determined what types of shows would be performed.

The price of admission led to conflict, and rising costs ultimately fueled the "Old Prices Riot" in 1809. Riots had accompanied

London theater for years, particularly when the prices first rose in 1762, but none to the degree of the "Old Prices Riot" (Donohue 52). The riot was only put to rest when the manager of the theater, John Philip Kemble, apologized publicly for the rising cost. The jump in price was caused in part by the cost of rebuilding the Covent Garden Theatre after it burned down the year before. James Boaden, a friend of Kemble, questioned the rebuilding of the Convent Garden Theatre, particularly the addition of extra boxes that were exclusive and private in a way that didn't exist before. Rioters also didn't agree with the privacy of these boxes, while others suggested the privacy promoted public debauchery, solely for the "privileged order" (Donohue 53). Overall, the theater had financial troubles that stretched across the decades. Costs were too high and admission increases caused social unrest. Drury Lane was lucky to have finished the year in black (Donohue 26).

The Monk Alive Today

Despite the thriving world of English theater in the late eighteenth and early nineteenth centuries, few well remembered works come from this period. The plays in this collection are unearthed from a forgotten part of theater history, one that is often overlooked because many plays were drawn from novels rather than being fully original works. In many ways, however, such plays mirror movies today, the majority of which are based on popular works of fiction and non-fiction. The recent film adaptation of Lewis' novel, *Le Moine,* created a bridge between the centuries and stands as an example of the mimicry of today's cinema. Directed by Dominik Moll, *Le Moine* graced the French and Spanish screens in 2011. It was met with mediocre reviews; some thought the cinematography was beautiful, while others felt there were many lapses in the plot (IMDb). While the adaptations of *The Monk* have not been the most popular, the original novel they imitate marks an important time in history, a time of questioning faith, liberty, and personal morals. The very things we may find ourselves questioning today.

Bibliography

Baker, David Erskine, Isaac Reed and Stephen Jones. *Biographia Dramatica; or, a Companion to the Playhouse*. London: Longman, Hurst, Rees, Orme, and Brown. 1812. Print.

Coleridge, Samuel Taylor. "Review of Lewis's *The Monk* (1797)." *Gothic Readings*. Ed. Rictor Norton. New York: Leicester University Press, 2000. Print.

Donohue, Joseph. *Theatre in the Age of Kean*. Totowa: Rowman and Littlefield, 1975. Print.

IMDb. Internet Movie Database: Amazon Company. 2010. Web. 22 March 2015.

Hamm, Larry R. "Matthew Gregory Lewis." *British Fantasy and Science-Fiction Writers Before World War I*. Ed. Darren Harris-Fain. Detroit: Bruccoli Clark Layman Book, 1997. Print.

Lewis, Matthew G. *The Monk*. New York: Barnes and Nobles Inc, 2009. Print.

Macdonald, D.L. "Matthew Gregory Lewis." *British Reform Writers, 1789-1832*. Eds. Gary Kelly and Edd Applegate. Detroit: Bruccoli Clark Layman Book, 1996. Print.

Mathias, Thomas James. "The Pursuits of Literature, or What You Will (1794-7)." *Gothic Readings*. Ed. Rictor Norton. New York: Leicester University Press, 2000. Print.

Watt, James. *Contesting the Gothic: Fiction, Genre and Cultural Conflict, 1764–1832*. New York: Cambridge University Press, 2004. Print.

Timeline

1660 King Charles is restored to the English throne; theaters are re-opened

1663 Thomas Killigrew orders the Theatre Royal in Bridges Street, predecessor of the Theatre-Royal, to be built

1672 Theatre Royal in Bridges Street burns down

1674 The theatre is rebuilt; renamed Theatre Royal in DruryLane

1737 The Licensing Act censors the British stage

1764 Horace Walpole publishes the first Gothic, *The Castle of Otranto*

1775 Matthew Gregory Lewis is born on July 9

1789 The Storming of the Bastille marks the beginning of the French Revolution

1794 G. G. and J. Robinson publish Ann Radcliffe's *Mysteries of Udolpho*

1794 Richard Brinsley Sheridan, owner of Theatre Royal in Drury Lane, tears down the theatre and rebuilds a bigger one

1796 Joseph Bell publishes first edition of Lewis' *The Monk* anonymously in March

1796 Bell publishes second edition of *The Monk* in October, and Lewis signs this edition with his full name

1797 Ann Radcliffe publishes Gothic Romance, *The Italian*

1797 Charles Farley's "Airs, Glees, And Chorusses In A New Grand Ballet Pantomime Of Action, Called Raymond And Agnes; Or The Castle Of Lindenbergh" is performed at the Theatre-Royal Covent-Garden

1798 Bell publishes fourth edition of *The Monk*, in which Lewis removes all offensive language

1799 James Boaden's "Aurelio and Miranda" is performed at the Theatre-Royal Covent-Garden

1818 Lewis dies at sea on May 14

1825 Boaden's popular work "Life of Kemble" is published

1827 Boaden publishes "Life of Mrs. Siddons"

1841 J. Clements publishes "Raymond and Agnes or the Bleeding Nun" for Lewis

1897 Bram Stoker publishes *Dracula*

2011 Dominik Moll directs *Le Moine*, an adaptation of *The Monk* that hits French and Spanish theaters

RAYMOND AND AGNES; THE TRAVELLERS BENIGHTED; OR, THE BLEEDING NUN OF LINDENBERG[1]

---

1 The source of this play is the acting copy from Cumberland's British Theatre, number 298. This edition is ascribed to Matthew Gregory Lewis, but Henry William Grosette is generally considered to be the author. I have not included George Daniel's "Remarks" on the play, for they are little more than plot summary. Finally, I have silently corrected inconsistent abbreviations and spellings of names, and other printer's errors.

Cast of the Characters,

As performed at the Theatres Royal, London.

	Covent Garden	*English Opera*
Don Felix	Mr. Cooper	Mr. Rowbotham
Don Raymond (his Son)	Mr. F. Vining	Mr. Webster
Theodore (Servant to Raymond)	Mr. F. Suttion	Mr. Brown
Conrad (a Domestic of Linden-berg Castle)	Mr. Sutton	Mr. Walbourn
Baptista (Banditti)	Mr. O. Smith	Mr. Salter
Robert (Banditti)	Mr. Grimaldi	Mr. T. P. Cooke
Jaques (Banditti)	Mr. T. Blanchard	Mr. Gouriet
Claude (Banditti) (a Postillion)	Mr. Turnour	Mr. Fisher
Marco (Master of an Hotel, and in League with the Banditti)	Mr. T. Matthews	Mr. Smith
Agnes	Miss Cawse	Miss Love
Cunegonde (her Governante)	Mrs. Davenport	Mrs. Grove
Sister Ursula	Miss Smith	Mrs. Jerrold
Marguerette (Wife of Baptista)	Mrs. W. Vining	Mrs. Chatterley
The Bleeding Nun	Miss Nicoll	Mrs. Shaw

SCENE—Spain.

COSTUME

DON FELIX.—Brown Spanish doublet and breeches—rich spangled cloak—russet shoes,[1] with rosettes.

DON RAYMOND.—Light blue velvet and silver tunic—white vest and tights—russet boots—ruff[2]—sword—black velvet hat, with white ostrich feathers.

THEODORE.—White kerseymere[3] doublet,[4] vest, and pantaloons,[5] trimmed with blue satin and black velvet binding—sword—russet boots—black hat and feathers.

CONRAD.—Yellow doublet, trunks, and vest, trimmed with blue and red binding—blue hose—russet boots—collar and hat to match.

BAPTISTA.—Brown tunic, vest, and trunks—red hose—russet shoes—gray wig—black hat and feathers—dagger, &c.

ROBERT.—Plum-coloured ditto.

JAQUES.—Iron-gray ditto.

CLAUDE.—Blue jacket—yellow vest—leather breeches[6]—large French boots—glazed[7] hat—hand-whip.

---

1 *russet*: Of boots or shoes: Made of leather which has not been blackened; tan, brown (OED).

2 *ruff*: An article of neck-wear, usually consisting of starched linen or muslin arranged in horizontal flutings and standing out all round the neck (OED).

3 *kerseymere*: A twilled fine woollen cloth of a peculiar texture (OED).

4 *doublet*: A close-fitting body-garment, with or without sleeves, worn by men from the 14th to the 18th centuries (OED).

5 *pantaloons*: A tight-fitting kind of trousers fastened with ribbons or buttons below the calf, or, later, by straps passing under the boots, which were introduced late in the 18th c., and began to supersede knee-breeches (OED).

6 *breeches*: distinguished from *trousers* by coming only just below the knee (OED).

7 *glazed*: Having a smooth shining surface (OED).

MARCO.—Salmon-coloured doublet, vest, and trunks, trimmed with blue and black binding, and bell buttons—blue hose—russet shoes—collar—hat and feathers to match.

AGNES.—*First dress*: White satin slip, over a white leno[1] dress—white hat and feathers—white satin shoes. *Second dress*: Same as the Bleeding Nun.

CUNEGONDE.—Old-fashioned bottle-green dress, with point-lace trimming—kerchief and apron—witches'-cut hat—high-heeled shoes.

URSULA.—Monastic black dress, with a large white covering or cap for the head.

MARGUERETTE.—Dark-blue stuff[2] body, petticoat, &c., trimmed with red binding—dark shoes—a blue ribbon run through the hair.

THE BLEEDING NUN.—White muslin—beads, cross, and dagger.

---

1 *leno*: A kind of cotton gauze, used for caps, veils, curtains, etc. (OED).

2 *stuff*: A woollen fabric (OED).

RAYMOND AND AGNES

OR, THE BLEEDING NUN.

ACT I.

SCENE I.—*A Gothic Library—a table, with pens, ink, &c.* MUSIC.—DON RAYMOND *discovered seated,* C., *reading,* THEODORE *attending,* L.

Ray. Books—sweet companions of my retirement, equally my delight and solace, farewell!—The commands of a much-honoured parent tears me from you now. Ah! shall I meet in that gay world companions at once so innocent and so instructive?

The. Oh, yes, sir, if you like, you may meet with whole folios of them, perhaps to the full as innocent, and certainly much more entertaining.

Ray. What, than books, sirrah?

The. Yes, signor, living books; for instance, woman, that lovely index, in which, though the student may sometimes discover a few errata, yet he is always sure to find those beauties which compose that sublime and wondrous work, called Nature.

Ray. Well said, Theodore; you improve, man.

The. Why, yes, signor; converse with the ladies does improve a man. O' my conscience! they can instruct better than your Homers, Virgils, Alexanders the Great, or any other of your heathen Greek poets.

Ray. [*Rising.*] Hush! here comes my father.

MUSIC.—*Enter* DON FELIX, R.

Fel. Raymond, my son, all is now in readiness for your departure; the hour is arrived when, for the first time, you quite your paternal roof without a guide, without a protector.

The. Then I am not to accompany my dear young signor?

Fel. Why, how now? what ails thee, knave?

The. Nothing, my lord; only I have a kind of moisture in my eyes, and a strange sort of choking in my throat, that's all.

Fel. Psha!—Most certainly, Theodore, thou shalt accompany my son.

The. The pray, signor, do not say Don Raymond will be without a protector. I'm not sufficiently acquainted with the road we are going, to be his guide, certainly; but should he stand in need of protection, depend upon it, signor, I will give it him.

Fel. I thank thy honest zeal, Theodore; it shall not be forgotten. [*Giving Raymond a purse.*] My son, here are two thousand pistoles;[1] they will amply supply your wants for some months;—when they are on the decline, fear not to draw upon me for more.

The. If he should, signor, I'll put him in remembrance of it.

Fel. But I have one request to make, Raymond; 'tis that you conceal your name and dignity. As Raymond, Count de la Cisternas, you would everywhere be received with respect and adulation; but that attention would be paid to your rank, not to your worth. Now, as Alphonso D'Alvarada, the name I mean you to assume, you must rely upon your own merits for a favourable reception from the world.

1 *pistole*: a Spanish gold coin worth a little less than a British pound. Thus, 2000 pistoles is more money than a common laborer would have made in a lifetime.

Ray. I hope, sir, I shall deserve your good opinion.—Your commands shall be religiously obeyed.

Fel. You alone, Theodore, shall accompany my son; I can depend upon your attachment and fidelity.

The. I have served him from my cradle, signor, and never yet failed in my duty; and if you find me changed on our return, I will give you leave to hang me up in a cage at the chateau, and show me as a travelled monster.

Fel. No more professions; we waste time. The carriage waits which is to bear you hence; come, my son, you must away. [*Music.—Exeunt,* R.]

SCENE II.—*A Street in Madrid—large gates leading to a Convent,* L. *3d.* E.—*a large hotel, with a balcony window over the door,* R. S. E.

Enter CUNEGONDE *and* CONRAD, R.

Cun. (C.) Holy St. Hilda! what a distressing journey have we had! I declare the Baron and Baroness Lindenberg have no more respect for the feelings of their friends, than if they imagined they were made of rock marble; while, Heaven knows, I have not one grain of adamant in my composition. [*Striking Conrad with her cane.*] Why, how you stand, lout! Am I, after my fatigue, to expire in the street for want of refreshment? Why do you not knock at the door? [*Conrad goes towards the hotel,* R.] Why, what are you about, sirrah?—Why do you not do as I order you?

Con. (R.) I'm going, madam, if you'll only give me time.

Cun. Holy St. Bridget! did I bid you go to the hotel, sirrah?

Con. You said you wanted refreshment.

Cun. Grant me patience! and you thought I should go to a tavern for it? Do you imagine such a place fit for the immaculate Cunegonde, principal domestic to the Baron and Baroness Lindenberg, and governante to their niece, the young and beautiful Agnes?

Con. I'm sure I do not know, madam.

Cun. Do not know!—Dolt! knock at the gates of the convent!

Con. Yes, madam. [*Crosses and knocks at the convent gates.*]

Enter URSULA, *the Porteress, from the gates,* L. *3d.* E.—*Cunegonde and Ursula salute each other ceremoniously.*

Cun. Holy sister, I wish to speak with the pious matron of St. Clare;—deliver this letter to her, and inform her that I am deputed by the Baron and Baroness of Lindenberg to take home their niece, the boarder Agnes.

Urs. The inhabitants of the convent are at present occupied in some religious duties in honour of our patroness, the holy St. Clare. If you will enter my apartment, as soon as they are finished, you shall be introduced to our pious mother.

Cun. Willingly, good sister. Follow us, Conrad!

Urs. Your pardon: the servant must not enter;—I am shocked at the idea of a man's profaning by his presence our holy walls.

Cun. Holy sister, pardon my inexperience. I respect the purity of your sentiments: ah! how much they accord with my own! [*Conrad being close at her elbow,* R., *she pushes him away.*] Conrad, stand further off, lest we should be contaminated by your touch! Wait for me in the street. [*Exeunt Ursula and Cunegonde through the convent gates—Conrad retires up,* R.]

Enter DON RAYMOND, R., *followed by* THEODORE, *carrying a portmanteau.*

Ray. (L.C.) At length we are arrived in Madrid.—Knock at the door of that hotel; I wish for a little refreshment.

The. [*Going to the hotel,* R. S. E., *and knocking at the door.*] And a large quantity would not be amiss for your faithful servant, Theodore. They say sorrow is dry; mine has made me hungry, too.

Ray. And, pray, what grief weighs so heavy upon your spirits?

The. Love, signor—love for my little black-eyed Annette! Ah! the very last time I met her, in the long cypress walk by moonlight, at the back of the chateau, she smiled, and said to me—

Enter MARCO *from the hotel,* R. S. E.

Mar. (R. C.) Who the devil was it that knocked at my door?

The. (C.) Oh, no! that was not what she said!

Ray. (L. C.) Landlord, I require some refreshment; and can you obtain for me a guide to conduct us through the forest to the next post?

Mar. Certainly I can, signor. If you will only give yourself the trouble to walk into my house, I will place before you wine fit for an emperor, and bring you the king of honest fellows for a guide.

Ray. Lead the way, then. [*Music.—Exeunt into the hotel,* R. S. E.]

Enter CUNEGONDE, AGNES, *and* URSULA, *through the convent gates,* L. *3d* E. —*Conrad remains,* R. U. E..

Cun. (R. C.) Nay, nay, young lady, cheer up! do not let your spirits be so depressed at parting with your holy mother;—recollect the kindness of your aunt and uncle, the Baroness and Baron of Lindenberg, and the pleasures that await you in their magnificent castle. [*Raymond appears in the balcony of the hotel.*]

Agnes. (C.) True, good Cunegonde; but to the dear abbess of St. Clare I owe the affection of a daughter: she has to me supplied the place of that mother whom I lost in infancy. Can I, then, part with her, perhaps for ever, without regret? And you, good mother Ursula, never will your poor Agnes forget your kindness. Farewell!

Urs. Farewell, my child; and may the Holy Virgin, in her own good time, wean you from the sinful delights of this world, and return you for ever to the peaceful solitude of St. Clare! Farewell! [*Raymond disappears from the balcony.*]

Cun. Adieu, dear mother! and when a few more years are passed over my head, I, too, may leave the temptations of mankind, and take the vows of eternal virginity within the walls of St. Clare. [*Music.—Agnes and Cunegonde take an affectionate leave of Ursula, who exits through the convent gates, closing them after her.*] Conrad, follow us, but keep at a respectful distance. [*Exeunt with Agnes,* R., *followed by Conrad.*]

Re-enter RAYMOND *from the hotel.*

Ray. [*Looking after Agnes.*] What a divinity! what a shape! how sweet the expression of her full dark eyes!—Lovely Agnes! never shall I forget this interesting moment. I have heard my father mention the Baron Lindenberg as an acquaintance of his youthful days. [*Calling.*] What, ho! landlord!

Re-enter MARCO *from the hotel,* R. S. E.

Pray, landlord, where is situated the chateau of the Baron de Lindenberg?

Mar. A few leagues hence, signor; on the borders of the forest which you are going to cross.

Ray. How fortunate! Is the guide ready?

Mar. He is waiting your honour's commands.

Ray. Send him to me with my servant. I must instantly depart.

Mar. [*Calling off.*] Hollo! Claude! Claude!

Enter CLAUDE *from the hotel, habited as a postilion, with a large stiletto in his girdle, followed by* THEODORE.

Here is the gentleman who requires your sevices. [*Marco eyes Raymond with marked suspicion.*]

Ray. [*To Claude.*] I wish you to guide us through the neighbouring forest; the road, I'm told, is both intricate and dangerous: do you know it sufficiently to conduct us safely?

Claude. (R.C.) Aye, noble signor; I have travelled every part of the forest at all hours for these last thirty years; and were it so dark that you could not see your hand before you, I would engage not to take you an inch out of the way.

Ray. 'Tis well. [*Going up to Theodore,* C.] We will depart this instant.

Claude. [*Apart to Marco.*] These are a couple of gudgeons,[1] whom it will not take much trouble to delude.—By their appearance, they seem to have more money than brains. [*To Raymond.*] This way, if you please; the chaise is quite ready, my lord. [*Music.—Exeunt Claude, Raymond, and Theodore,* R.—*Marco into the hotel,* R. S. E..]

SCENE III.—*A thick Forest—Night.*

Enter BAPTISTA, *listening for travelers,* R.

Bap. Not the least sound strikes my ear;—where can my comrades loiter? It is now night, and since the day has closed, not one of my band has met my sight. I am left, like the wolf, to prowl alone and seek my prey: like him, I am driven from mankind, and, like him, make reprisals upon those whose ill fortune throws them in my power. [*A whistle is heard without.—he answers it.*] Hark! [*Music.—A smack of a whip, and crash of a chaise breaking down, heard without,* L. —*Exit Baptista, rejoicing,* R.]

Enter CLAUDE, RAYMOND, *and* THEODORE, L.

The. Oh, dear! oh, dear!—Well, of all the unlucky accidents which could befall us, sure this is the most unfortunate! Our chaise to break down with us in the middle of a thick

1 *gudgeon*: One that will bite at any bait or swallow anything: a credulous, gullible person (OED). Literally, a gudgeon is a small fresh-water fish.

forest at midnight! Had I been the guide myself, I could not have done a more foolish thing.

Claude. It was no fault of mine; I have not brought you out of the road; and if the axle-tree of the chaise thinks proper to give way, am I to blame for that?

Ray. A truce with altercation;—since the accident has happened, think how we best may remedy it. Is there any village near the spot where we may hope to get the carriage repaired?

Claude. No, signor; the nearest place is that we have just left; and it is impossible to drag the broken vehicle so far in the dark.

The. What can be done? Oh, I have it! If your honour will let him mount one of the mules, he may endeavour to find his way back to Madrid, and return with assistance.

Claude. I should, perhaps, lose myself in the intricacies of the forest; and your master, waiting here for me, be compelled to pass the night in the open air.

The. That he must do, I fear, at all events; and my proposal is the only chance we have of escape.

Claude. No, no; not so bad off as that, neither. A few paces hence there is a wood-cutter's cottage;—the wood-cutter is a friendly, honest fellow, and I dare say he will willingly give us a night's lodging.

The. What a stupid fellow you must be to puzzle us so, then! Really, my good friend, your skull is of a very comfortable thickness. Why didn't you think of this before?

Claude. So I did; but as my friend is poor, and his accommodations not what the signor has been used to, I thought he would not accept the offer.

Ray. If your friend will afford us shelter till the morning, however humble it may be, I shall both thank and reward him for it.

Claude. He will look for no reward, signor: he is a well-meaning fellow; and whatever it is in his power to give, you will be heartily welcome to.

The. St. Antony be praised! Then we have escaped an adventure for this night, however.

Claude. [*Aside.*] Perhaps you have met with one you little expected. [*To Raymond.*] Follow me, signor. [*Exeunt,* R.]

SCENE IV.—*A Wood—a Cottage,* L. C. F.—*a candle seen burning in the chamber window.*

MUSIC.—*Enter* BAPTISTA, R., *but seeing the travellers advancing, he hurries into the cottage, and closes the door after him.*

Enter CLAUDE, RAYMOND, *and* THEODORE, R.

Claude. Here, signor, is the house I spoke of; and, see, my honest friend has not yet retired to rest, for the candle is still burning in his cottage,

Ray. Knock, Theodore; the wind blows sharp and cold. [*Theodore crosses at the back, and knocks at the cottage door.*]

Claude. (R.) Ay, ay, signor, I warrant honest Baptista has a blazing fire, which will soon warm your benumbed joints. There is no scarcity of wood in this part of the world.

The. (L.) You may say that with justice: we are now lost in one, through choosing a guide, whose head, I suspect, is made of the same materials.

Ray. (C.) Peace, Theodore, and knock again.

The. I will try again; but I believe the people are all dead, or fast asleep. [*Knocking.*] Hollo! within there!

Baptista. [*Putting his head out of the window.*]—Hollo! without there!—Who knocks so loud a this late hour?

Claude. (C.) It is I, friend Baptista. A gentleman, whose carriage has broken down in the forest, wishes for a night's lodging: can you accommodate him and his servant?

Bap. Ah, is it you, honest Claude? Wait a moment, and I'll be with you. [*Retires from the window.*]

Claude. I told you, signor, we should find a hearty welcome.

Re-enter BAPTISTA *from the cottage,* (L. C. F.)

Bap. [*To Claude.*] Ah, my old friend! I'm glad to see you. [*To Raymond, with affected cordiality.*] Walk in, signor; you are welcome to what refreshment my poor hovel can afford. I hope you will excuse my not opening the door before; but this forest is infested with a desperate gang of banditti, and I was fearful it might be some of them, who had perceived a light through my cottage window. Truly, signor, you were fortunate in having my friend Claude with you, or you would have run some risk of falling into their clutches. But come, enter, signors; believe me, you are heartily welcome. [*Exeunt into the cottage.*]

SCENE V.—*Inside of a mean Cottage—stairs,* R. *3d* E.—*a fire-place,* L. S. E.—*a door,* R. F.—*a cupboard,* L. C. F.—*a couch, with an infant asleep,* R.S. E.—*a table,* L. C.—*chairs and stools.*

MARGUERETTE *discovered watching the child,* R.

Mar. Sweet babe! thou sleep'st unconscious of the pangs which rend thy mother's heart. Alas! that I should be driven to curse the father of my child—a fiend unworthy of the name of man! By brutal force he made he his; by force detains me here, to witness deeds of horror, that harrow up my soul! [*Kneeling.*] All gracious Heaven, hear my prayer! For three long years have I groaned beneath a weight of guilt: oh! release me from it, and solemnly do I promise to dedicate this infant to thy service! Oh! may the piety of his future life wash away the infamy of his birth! [*Music.—She kisses the infant, and slowly ascends the stairs,* R. *3d* E.]

Enter BAPTISTA, RAYMOND, *and* THEODORE, *carrying a portmanteau,* R. D. F.

Bap. You see, signor, my hovel, as I told you, is poor, but comfortable; and such as it is, you are welcome.—Pray be seated, and my wife shall bring you some refreshment. [*Calling.*] Marguerette! Marguerette, I say!

Re-enter MARGUERETTE, R.

Mar. [*Aside.*] Ha! another victim!

Bap. Why, what are you about, wife? Don't you see that we have strangers? Come, stir about, and get something ready for supper; the gentleman is half famished; and if my old friend Claude had not brought him here, he must have passed the night in the forest.

Mar. [*Sorrowfully.*] Would to heaven that he had passed it anywhere but beneath this roof!

Bap. [*Angrily.*] How!

Ray. Your pardon; let not my presence create dispute. If our company, my good friend, be displeasing to your wife, we will instantly quit your hospitable roof.

Bap. No, no, signor, heed her not; she is crabbed and hasty, but she will make you welcome notwithstanding—will you not, my old lass! [*Apart to her.*] Another word, and [*Showing a dagger.*] I will use effectual means to silence you!

Mar. [*Aside.*] What shall I do? My soul sickens with horror at the frequent scenes of blood which stain this guilty spot!

Bap. Where can Robert and Jaques loiter? The night is dark, and I am apprehensive that they may meet with evil-disposed people in the forest.

Mar. Oh, fear not: they cannot meet with any worse disposed than themselves.

Bap. [*Apart to her, fierecely.*] Marguerette! [*To Raymond.*] They are my sons, signor, by a former marriage; therefore my wife esteems them not, though they are two as fine young men as any this day in Spain;—rather rough and unpolished, to be sure, but honest.

The. [*Gaping.*] Yaw! yaw!

Bap. You seem sleepy, signor. You can lie down on the bed while my wife prepares supper, if you choose it.

The. With all my heart.

Bap. Wife, show the young man to his chamber—the small one: [*Significantly.*] you understand me?

Mar. I am busy.

Bap. Well, if you are, you still have time enough to do as I order you. Come! [*Music.—He gives Marguerette a lamp, and she ascends the stairs sullenly, followed by Theodore.*]

Enter ROBERT *and* JAQUES, R. D. F.—*they start on seeing Raymond, and place their hands on their daggers—Baptista throws himself between them, to prevent Raymond's observing them.—Re-enter* MARGUERETTE *down the stairs.*

Bap. (C.) My sons, signor; they were somewhat surprised at seeing a stranger, but they will be proud to pay their respects to you.

Ray. [*Coming forward, and sitting* L.] I am glad they have arrived in safety; though I perceive they travel well armed.

Rob. (R. C.) Why, yes, signor; it is a precaution we are used to, though I believe needless; for I never yet was molested.

Jaques. (R. *corner.*) May be so; but no person can tell what may befall him, even when he thinks himself most secure. [*Music.—Raymond dozes—Robert goes cautiously behind, and attempts to stab him—Marguerette advances quickly, and prevents him.*]

Mar. [*Shaking Raymond on the shoulder.*] Signor, you are fatigued: come, I will conduct you to your chamber.

Ray. I thank you;—an hour's rest will refresh me.

Mar. And in that time your supper will be ready for you. Come, signor. [*Music.—She takes the candle, and prepares to show him the way, when Robert, who has observed her with suspicion, snatches the candle from her.*]

Rob. Mother, I will show the gentleman to his room; do you remain below. [*To Raymond.*] Come, signor; lie down and refresh yourself, and before your supper is ready, my life on't you will be quite another man. [*Music.—Marguerette slips up the stairs unperceived—Raymond ascends, lighted by Robert—Exeunt Baptista and Jaques* R. D. F.]

SCENE VI.—*A Wood, and outside of Baptista's Cottage, as before.*

Enter BAPTISTA *and* JAQUES *from the cottage, L. C. F.*

Jaq. I am doubtful of Marguerette, father; methinks she seems but little disposed to aid our intentions.

Bap. True; but she dare not counteract them; for she knows her own life would be the forfeit. You say there are two thousand pistoles in the portmanteau?

Jaq. So the servant boasted at the inn.

Bap. Well, then, success to the division of the booty!

Jaq. Division!—Why, is the landlord to have any share of it?

Bap. To be sure he is; his assistance is necessary to—

Jaq. Why, I rather think it too bad that we are to have all the trouble and risk, and he all the comfort and profit.

Bap. For shame, son! how can you be so selfish! We have bound ourselves by oath, and we have never been mean enough to violate it. Consider our honour;—let us always act with justice and humanity. By the bye, while Robert is dispatching the master, I think you had better go and rob the servant;—it will be pastime till supper is ready.

Jaq. But about this division—I can't see—

Bap. Silence, boy!—Would you bring disgrace upon our family? Go and do as I order you. [*Exeunt into the cottage.*]

SCENE VII.—*A miserable Chamber in the Cottage—a door,* R. F.—*a window, with iron bars,* C. F.—*a bed,* L. *3d* E., *with a chair and table close to it.*

MARGUERETTE *discovered looking it at the door.*

Mar. What can I do? how can I preserve him? They are ascending the stairs: I must be quick. I dare not show myself. Ha! the pillow! [*She draws off the case, and the pillow appears bloody.*] Should he perceive it, stained as it is with the blood of numerous victims, who have fallen by Robert's murderous hands, it will at least put him on his guard.

Rob. [*Without,* R. U. E.] This way, signor. [*Marguerette conceals herself behind the bed curtains.*]

Enter ROBERT *and* RAYMOND, D. F.

Rob. [*Placing the light on the table.*] Here is your bed, signor; you will not be the first stranger that has slept in it—aye, and soundly, too.

Ray. I do not doubt it. If you will retire, I will endeavour to get a little repose.

Rob. Aye, aye, I will leave you; and if you please to give me your sword, I will take care of it for you.

Ray. My sword!

Rob. Aye, your sword: you can have no use for it while you sleep.

Ray. [*Pointedly.*] True; and, while I sleep, what use can you have for it?

Rob. [*Aside.*] Confusion! [*Hesitating.*] Me!—Oh, ah!—me! Certainly, none. I offered out of civility to take care of it for you: if you do not choose to part with it, that's another thing.

Ray. I certainly shall not part with it.

Rob. [*Crossing to* R.] Oh, very well; as you please; we are in no want of arms, though I think your refusal has an odd appearance;—but do as you like. [*Exit,* D. F.]

Ray. I like not the youth who has just now left me; his ferocious glance chills my blood. The remembrance, too, of the lovely Agnes employs my busy fancy. [*Lying down on the bed.*] I will endeavour, by a short repose, to chase away my gloomy apprehensions.

MUSIC.—*Re-enter* ROBERT, D. F.—*he advances cautiously towards the bed with a drawn dagger—Marguerette, from behind the curtains, shakes Raymond, who starts up.*

Ray. [*Leaping forward, and seizing Robert by the collar.*] How is this?—What has brought you here?

Rob. [*Panic struck, and hesitatingly.*] I—I—I came to fetch—the lamp.

Ray. [*Firmly.*] Let it remain.

Rob. Cannot you sleep in the dark?

Ray. I do not choose to be left without a light.

Rob. It's wanted below.

Ray. Then I will go down, too.

Rob. No, no, stay where you are; my mother is busy, and don't want to be troubled with you. She sent me for the lamp, but she must do without it. [*Aside, going.*] Curses light on him! [*Exit,* D.F. *Raymond follows Robert to the door.*]

Mar. [*Coming forward,* C.] The blood-thirsty villain!

Ray. [*Starting.*] Ha! how did you enter?

Mar. Hush! one word, and you are lost for ever! I wish to save you. Examine the pillow of your bed. [*Going towards the door.*] The wretch who has just left you—

Re-enter ROBERT, D. F., *meeting her—they are mutually struck with surprise.*

Rob. What brought you here?

Mar. [*Faltering.*] I—I came—to—to—

Rob. To do what?—Why do you hesitate? [*With savage impatience.*] What was your errand here?

Mar. Why do you ask? [*A pause—then recollecting herself, and drawing a cap from her bosom.*] See you not this cap? I brought it for the stranger.

Rob. [*Snatching it from her.*] It may be so. You are wanted below. [*Throwing it to Raymond.*] There's the cap. [*To Marguerette.*] Now, come with me; I know not any business which you can have with the stranger.—Come, I say! [*Exit, forcing her out,* D. F. *Music.—Raymond hurries to the bed, seizes the pillow, and seems horror-stricken.*]

Ray. [*Drawing his sword, and rushing to the window.*] Ha! the window secured! Then am I in a den of robbers! but my good sword is still left for my protection, and I will not part with life unless it be dearly purchased. Footsteps again! I will feign to sleep, yet keep good guard against the assassin's steel! [*Music.—He goes softly to the door, and listens—then retires to the bed, and lays down upon his sword.*]

Re-enter ROBERT, D. F. , *followed by* MARGUERETTE, *watching him—he advances to the bed, and is about to stab Raymond, when Marguerette overturns the table, and retreats hastily behind the door.*

Ray. [*Starting up, and holding his sword to Robert's breast.*] Why am I thus continually disturbed?—What can be the reason of this second intrusion?

Rob. [*Surlily.*] Supper is on the table: if you wish for any, come down; if you don't, stay here and sleep.

Ray. That I find to be impossible: you will not leave me a moment to myself.

Rob. I come not without a cause. I will carry your lamp and your sword for you.

Ray. I have already told you I do not choose to part with it.

Rob. You are strangely suspicious, methinks. If you will carry one, then you may carry both. I shall not wait here for you till the supper is cold. [*Exit,* D. F.]

Ray. How horrible is my situation! Their intent is clear—they aim at my life! How shall I act?

Mar. [*Coming forward,* R.] Signor, your life is for the present preserved: betray not the least suspicion, or you will instantly be sacrificed.

Ray. My generous preserver! how is it I meet you an associate with such monsters?

Mar. There is no time for explanation: necessity, not choice, has made me what I am. Yet will I save your life, or perish with you. [*Taking up the lamp.*] Follow me! [*Exeunt,* D. F., *Marguerette encouraging Raymond to follow her.*]

SCENE VIII.—*A thick Wood.—Moonlight.*

Enter CUNEGONDE *and* AGNES, L., *followed by* CONRAD *and* MARCO.

Cun. Holy St. Bridget, defend me! Sure our troubles are never to have an end! Who could have suspected such a misfortune? Why, the road from the convent of St. Clare to the castle of Lindenberg is as plain as the nose on one's face; and yet this stupid, deaf fool of a guide contrived to lose it!

Agnes. Patience, dear Cunegonde!—By your loud complaints, you only aggravate the danger of our situation.—Should the forest, as we are informed, be the haunt of banditti—

Cun. Banditti! [*Crying.*] Oh, dear! oh, dear!—O that I had dedicated myself to a life of perpetual virginity in the holy convent of St. Clare!—Then should I have escaped the dangers with which my innocence is surrounded! [*To Marco.*] And you, sirrah, what can you say for yourself?—How can we get out of the dilemma you have brought us into?

Mar. [*To Conrad, affecting deafness.*] Eh? what?—Did her ladyship address herself to me?

Cun. Certainly her ladyship did. Was ever poor governante so plagued with idiots and knaves as myself?—And you, Conrad, why you're stupid—absolutely petrified. What is to be done? what course are we next to take?

Con. Really, madam, I cannot tell.

Mar. [*Aside.*] What can have become of the band?

Agnes. [*Looking off,* R.] Be of good heart, madam. I surely espied the form of a man passing down the close walk to the right.

Cun. [*Screaming.*] Ha! a man! a robber! Oh, holy St. Clare, protect me!—me, one of the most virtuous of thy votaries!—Oh, save me from his unhallowed touch! [*Clings round the neck of Conrad.*]

Enter CLAUDE, *with a dark lantern,* R.

Claude. [*Aside.*] Methought I heard female voices.—Ha! Marco here! Then I know my cue. [*Advancing.*] Who goes there? Ah, ladies! I entreat your pardon; but hearing voices, I feared it might be some, whose evil designs caused them to wander in the forest.

Cun. [*Trembling behind Conrad.*] Oh! oh! oh!

Agnes. We are wanderers through misfortune, not intention. Crossing the forest from Madrid to the castle of Lindenberg, our servant and guide have deviated from the path. If you can assist us in regaining the road, you shall be amply rewarded for your service.

Claude. That, lady, is not in my power; I am ignorant of the road you mention;—but there is an honest peasant, whose cottage stands but a few paces hence, who will not only give you shelter till the morning, but, for a trifling recompense, lead you beyond the intricacies of the forest.

Cun. [*Crossing to Claude.*] Oh! take us thither instantly, young man. You are the guardian angel sent to preserve my life!

Claude. Bless you, madam, I'm no angel!—I'm only a poor devil, who earns a livelihood by felling timber in the forest;—but I will conduct the young lady, if you have no objection. I suppose, madam, you are her mother.

Cun. What? mother? Pray, sir, look in my face, and tell me if there are any lines in it which indicate my being the mother of a girl like that?

Claude. I ask your pardon for the mistake, madam: I now perceive you are her grandmother.

Cun. Pooh! grandmother, indeed! at my time of life—in the blossom of my days! I am her governante, it is true, though there is very little difference in our ages.—But which path must we pursue to the cottage you mentioned?

Claude. That by which I came hither. If you please, I will return with you, and show you the spot.

Cun. With all my heart. Come, Lady Agnes. Mother, forsooth! We are in a hopeful situation, truly, with one guide as deaf as a post, and t'other as blind as a bat!

Claude. [*To Conrad.*] Come, comrade; bear the light, and on before us. [*Exeunt,* R., *Conrad taking the lantern, and lighting Agnes and Cunegonde, who are followed by Claude and Marco, making significant signs to each other.*]

SCENE IX.—*The Lower Room in Baptista's Cottage, as before.*

MUSIC.—BAPTISTA *and* JAQUES *discovered.*

Enter ROBERT *down the stairs,* R. *3d* E.

Bap. [*To Robert.*] What success, my lad?

Jaq. Is he dispatched?

Rob. No. I believe all the fiends of hell are in league against me. Curses on the officious Marguerette! She has more than once prevented me. Why did you not detain her below?

Bap. No matter. You will mar all by your impetuosity: slow and sure is my maxim. When he sleeps, it may be done without much difficulty.

Jaq. Hush! they come.

MUSIC.—*Enter* RAYMOND *down the stairs, followed by* MARGUERETTE, *carrying a lamp, which she places on a shelf.—A knocking is heard at the door,* R. F.—*Baptista opens it.*

Enter CLAUDE, *conducting in* AGNES *and* CUNEGONDE.

Bap. How now?

Ray. [*Aside.*] By all that's lovely! 'tis the very angel that I beheld from the hotel quitting the convent at Madrid!

Claude. Don't be alarmed, friend Baptista. This lady and her attendants have lost their road in the forest;—I fortunately chanced to meet with them, and assured them of finding a welcome at your cottage.

Bap. [*Hesitating.*] Why, yes; but you know we have already this gentleman and his servant;—our beds are full.

Agnes. How unfortunate!

Ray. Nay, gentle lady, let not that distress you: such accommodations as were meant for me, are at your service, if you will deign to accept them.

Agnes. Signor, I thank your courtesy.

Ray. Fair lady, I deserve no thanks. [*Leading her to the fire-place,* L.] It is the duty of man to forego his own comforts, to shield from distress a lovely woman.

Cun. Oh, holy St. Bridget! what a pain was there!—Oh, my poor head!—I have caught my death in this precious forest, [*Eyeing the table.*] and I dare say there is not a drop of cordial to be had for love or money.

Bap. I have a small bottle of fine cherry brandy, signora; perhaps a drop of that might relieve you.

Cun. Mercy!—Is there anything in my appearance to indicate that I would swallow such unholy liquor?

Bap. Unholy!—I wish every hole in my skin was full of it, for I always find it the best medicine; and there's nothing else to be got.

Cun. Well, the urgency of the case must plead my excuse; so you may just fill me a thimble full, and I will try to get it down.

Bap. [*Filling the glass, and handing it to her.*] That's right, signora; grapple with the spirit, and you will be sure to conquer it!

Cun. [*Drinking.*] Really, it is not so bad as I expected.

Bap. You had better have t'other glass. [*Handing it to her.*] Come, come signora, drink!—The psalm says, 'tis

> "A balm for ev'ry wound,—
>
> A cordial for our fears."[1]

Cun. Well, if you think so—[*Drinking.*] Oh, dear! my poor head is shattered into a thousand pieces!

Bap. A little rest will restore you; there is a bed ready.

Cun. The Virgin be praised!

1 from a popular hymn by Isaac Watts (1674-1748).

Bap. Wife, light this lady to her chamber. [*To Cunegonde.*] Would you like to take another glass, madam?

Cun. [*Going.*] St. Bridget forbid! [*Returning.*] Yet, in case I should be taken ill in the night, you may as well give me the bottle, to place by my bedside. The saints preserve you all, and give you a good night's rest! [*Music.—Exeunt Marguerette and Cunegonde up the stairs—the others all sit to supper at the table,* L., *and Marguerette returns.*]

Bap. Wife, bring me the bottle which is sealed with yellow wax.

Mar. [*Hesitating.*] With yellow?

Bap. Yes; you understand me?—Bring it, and instantly! [*She reluctantly gives it to him.*]

Mar. [*Apart to Raymond, passing him,* L.] Do not drink!

Bap. [*To Raymond.*] Come, signor, here is some champagne which I have had by me many years; I never bring it out but upon extraordinary occasions; and as your supper is course, this may help give it a relish. [*Music.—He pours out the wine—Agnes drinks, but Raymond, unseen, throws his upon the ground.*] Is it not most excellent, signor?

Ray. It is, indeed. Champagne is a wine to which I am extremely partial.

Bap. And I assure you, this has some very extraordinary virtues. [*To Agnes.*] I hope, madam, that you approve of it.

Agnes. [*Drowsily.*] It is excellent, yet rather powerful. [*She falls asleep.*]

Bap. I think it the better for that, madam. [*To Raymond.*] Have you travelled far, signor?

Ray. From a league on the other side of Madrid. [*Marguerette, unperceived by the banditti, motions Raymond to affect to sleep, which he does.*]

Bap. 'Tis well: the wine has taken effect.

Rob. [*Rising.*] I will dispatch him, then.

Bap. No; leave me to deal with the sleepers; they are sure work, and unable to make resistance. You, with Jaques and Claude, hasten to the forest, and endeavour to overpower the servants of the lady, who are with the carriage; lest they should come in the morning, and ask questions we should not like to answer.

Rob. Be it so. Come, lads. [*Music.—Exeunt Robert, Jaques, and Claude,* R. D. F.]

Mar. [*Shaking Raymond,* L.] Now! [*Baptista draws his dagger, and crosses quickly to Agnes, and as he is about to strike, Raymond starts up, and arrests his arm—they struggle—the dagger drops—Marguerette hastily snatches it up, stabs Baptista, and he falls.*]

Mar. [*Dropping on her knees.*] All gracious Powers! pronounce my pardon!—The villain sleeps in death!—Would he had fallen by any other hand! [*To Raymond, rising.*] Let us instantly away! flight alone can save us.

Ray. But should we meet the other villains in the forest—

Mar. Here, under the stairs, is a private way, which leads to a road quite contrary to the one the robbers have taken. [*Music.—Marguerette ascends the stairs, and returns with her infant, Theodore, and Cunegonde—she points out to Theodore the private passage under the stairs, who exits, followed by the others, Raymond carrying Agnes in his arms.*]

Re-enter ROBERT, JAQUES, *and* CLAUDE, R. D. F.

Rob. Confusion!—Everything conspires to cross us: the servants doubtless suspected us, or they would not have fled. I hope, at least, my father has made sure work with those he had in his power.

Jaq. [*Seeing the body of Baptista.*] 'Sdeath![1] what have we here? My father murdered!

Rob. Ha! where is the stranger? Marguerette shall dearly pay for this! [*Music.—He rushes up the stairs—Jaques and Claude kneel by the body of Baptista.*]

Rob. [*Descending the stairs.*] They have all escaped! let us instantly pursue them; they cannot be far from hence. I swear to follow them to the end of the world, and revenge the death of my father!

Jaq. We all swear to revenge his death, or fall in the attempt! [*Music.—They kneel, and cross their daggers over the body.*]

END OF ACT I

1 *'sdeath*: an oath, short for "God's death."

ACT II

SCENE I.—*Outside of the Gates of Lindenberg Castle—a window in the wall,* L. U. E.

MUSIC. —*Enter* RAYMOND, THEODORE, *and* MARGUERETTE, *through the gates, which are opened and closed by a servant.*

The. Well, I declare, I never was more civilly turned out of doors in all my life! We are like to make a hopeful journey of it. The first place we stop at, we are near having our throats cut; and at the second, ere we have well refreshed ourselves, we are turned out, and the gates barred against us, as if they thought we were going to cut theirs!

Ray. Agnes—dear Agnes! farewell! Come, Marguerette, you shall accompany me to my father's; he will take a pleasure in repaying the kindness you have shown his son. Trust me, you will not experience such ingratitude as we have received from yonder lord.

Mar. Don Alphonso, I only wish a safe conveyance to Strasbourg, where I have relations; I would not willingly give you further trouble.

Ray. That must not be. Allow me to show my gratitude, and, in some measure, make recompense to you for the injustice of others. [*A guitar is heard within the castle.*] Hark! [*A paper is lowered from the window,* L. U. E.] Ha! that is the window of Agnes' apartment! [*Taking up the paper, and reading.*] "*Don Alphonso,—To-morrow I am to be immured for life within the walls of a convent. My heart revolts at the idea of taking the veil; and I have no other alternative but to confide in your honour. At one o'clock at night I will leave my chamber, disguised as the Bleeding Nun; which will ensure the certainty of my escape. If you are sincere, meet me without the castle gates; if not, leave me to my fate.* —AGNES." Excellent device! Fear not, sweet Agnes! I will be punctual; and should our project be successful—

The. Oh, dear! oh, dear! —Why, surely, sir, the Lady Agnes is not going to have the temerity to personate the ghost? Holy St. Francis! even in the short space of time they suffered us to remain in the castle, I heard enough concerning her to make me keep at a respectful distance.

Ray. Take courage, Theodore!—My lovely spirit has nothing terrific about her;—and if borrowing the ghost's robes will answer the purpose of uniting two hearts who sincerely love each other, I shall ever bless the Bleeding Nun of Lindenberg! [*Exeunt*, R. S. E.]

SCENE II.—*A Wood—Night—Whistling heard without.*

Enter ROBERT, L., *and* JAQUES *and* CLAUDE, R.

Rob. Who goes there?

Jaq. Robert?

Rob. The same. Where is Claude?

Jaq. He is here.

Rob. Have you been successful?

Jaq. I have not discovered the least trace of them.

Claude. Nor I;—they are doubtless arrived ere now at the castle of Lindenberg. 'Tis my advice that we instantly proceed thither, and endeavour to way-lay the cavalier who has played us this scurvy trick.

Rob. It shall be so. We will each of us take a different road to the cavern; there we will repose for the night, and in the morning early hasten to the castle, where we will watch for the murderer of my father.

Jaq. We have sworn his destruction; nor shall Marguerette, or her child, escape our vengeance.

Rob. Hence, then; here we separate. To the cavern! This night our revenge shall sleep. [*Exeunt,* R. *and* L.]

SCENE III.—*Outside the Gates of Lindenberg Castle, as before.—Midnight.*

Enter RAYMOND *and* THEODORE, R.

Ray. Come, Theodore, let us have no cowardly fears now;—wait at a little distance, and when Agnes comes forth, we will join you. Away! remain alone, and be silent.

The. I must perforce; yet I would give one of my eyes for a companion to speak to, if it were only old Cunegonde, who, I dare say, is fast asleep in her warm, comfortable bed, and not even dreaming how we are employed. [*Exit,* L.—*The castle bell strikes one.*]

Ray. Hark!

Enter the BLEEDING NUN *through the gates—she crosses and exits,* R.—*Raymond follows her in ecstasy.*

Re-enter THEODORE, L.

The. I cannot abide to be alone in the dark at this time of night; my apprehensions are worse than reality.—Oh, dear! where can my master and the Lady Agnes be? Which way can they have gone? How did I miss them? [*Going,* R.]

Enter AGNES *from the castle, dressed as the Bleeding Nun.*

The. [*Falling on his knees,* C.] Holy St. Michael, preserve me!—Yonder comes the real ghost!—Oh! what would I give to be safe at home, and in a whole skin!

Agnes. [*Crossing to* L.] Ha! a man!—It is Alphonso's servant. Speak, Theodore; where is your master?

The. [*Groaning.*] Oh! oh!—From goblins and spectres, holy Virgin preserve me!

Agnes. [*Approaching him.*] Theodore, look up: it is me—Agnes. Where is your master?

The. [*Rising.*] Agnes!—Thanks be praised! It is the Lady Agnes, sure enough, and pure flesh and blood, instead of a withered skeleton!

Agnes. Where is Don Alphonso?

The. Why, has not your ladyship seen him? I left him but a few minutes since waiting for you.

Agnes. Accident prevented me leaving my chamber so soon as I intended; but surely he waited not so long, as to be out of patience?

The. My life upon it, madam, he is close at hand.

Agnes. This tardiness, at a moment when he knew my liberty was at stake, betrays an indifference to my fate that I expected not.

The. I will lead you to him instantly;—you may trust yourself with me without fear, my lady.

Agnes. I have not other resource. [*Aside, going.*] Alas! how has my imprudence involved me! [*Exeunt*, R.]

SCENE IV.—*A Front Wood.*

MUSIC.—*Enter the* BLEEDING NUN, L., RAYMOND *still following, and endeavouring to approach her—at each advance, the Nun presents a dagger to him—they finally cross, and exeunt* R.

SCENE V.—*A Cut and Back Wood—a mound*, C.

Enter the BLEEDING NUN *and* RAYMOND *through the wood*, R. U. E.—*Raymond, still supposing her to be Agnes, follows her till she gets on the mound*, C.—*as he approaches to embrace her, she vanishes, and a transparency rises on the mound with the following inscription:*—

"PROTECT THE CHILD OF THE MURDERED AGNES!"

Ray. Ye powers of mercy!—Yes, I swear to obey the injunctions! My Agnes, then, is the hapless orphan!—Alas! to what distress may not my absence at this moment expose her? Beatified[1] spirit! hear me renew the solemn vow to protect thy lovely child—the injured Agnes; and may I be happy or wretched as I keep my oath! [*Music.—Exit*, L.]

1 *beatified*: Declared to be in the enjoyment of heavenly bliss (OED). The Bleeding Nun in Lewis' novel, of course, is not beatified when Raymond first meets her.

SCENE VI.—*A Mountain Pass—a Cavern,* R. U. E.

JAQUES *and* CLAUDE *discovered watching.*

Enter ROBERT, L. U. E.

Rob. [*Looking off,* L.] Hasten and conceal yourselves. Yonder are two passengers descending into the vale;—climb the trees, and when they are within reach, drop and secure them. Quick! quick! [*They ascend the trees,* R. *and* L. U. E.]

Enter THEODORE, L., *leading* AGNES.

The. Nay, madam, cheer up; why so dejected? We shall soon reach the castle of Don Felix, my master's father. Then do not, lady, thus despair.

Agnes. Oh! I am sick at the heart! The absence of Don Raymond fills my mind with a thousand doubts and apprehensions. Alas! why did he conceal his name and rank? Had he avowed them to my uncle, I need not now have been a wanderer.

The. It was by the command of his father, lady, that he concealed it; and I shall incur his displeasure for breaking through his strict behests. But I could not bear to hear you doubt my master's honour; and I knew when you heard the name of Raymond, all your doubts must cease. Dishonour was never yet coupled with that name.

Agnes. Most true; yet still his continued absence fills my mind with serious alarm. [*The Robbers cautiously descend from the trees.*]

Rob. [*Apart to Jaques and Claude.*] Steady, boys! steady! Here are a couple of our runaways; they shall not now escape us.

The. Come, madam;—when we have passed yonder thicket, we shall see before us the spires of Madrid.

Rob. [*Crossing to them.*] Stand!

Agnes. [*Starting.*] Ha! robbers! Alas! for what am I reserved?

Rob. Lady, you may haply recollect us: we know our obligations to you, and doubt not but we will repay them.

The. We know likewise your kind intentions towards us; and therefore do not suppose you the least in our debt.

Rob. Silence, fool!—You are now within our power: if you again escape, it shall be our own fault. [*To Jaques and Claude.*] Drag them to the cave!

The. [*Drawing his sword.*] The first that approaches this lady shall make his way through my body! So, if ye are cowards enough to assail one man, come on, all of ye at once!

Rob. No; I alone will oppose you. Perhaps 'twas your hand that plunged the dagger into the heart of my father. Revenge will nerve mine in return!

The. Have at you, then!—Robber or devil, you shall find that Theodore is not easily to be conquered. [*Music.—They encounter—Jaques and Claude drag Agnes into the cavern,* R. U. E.—*Theodore and Robert exeunt, fighting,* R.]

Enter RAYMOND *and* MARGUERETTE, L.

Ray. It is in vain—no where can I behold her!—Agnes! dearest Agnes! what can be your fate?

Mar. Calm yourself, signor: the absence of your servant proves that he is with her, and fear not but Theodore will protect her.

Ray. Alas! may she not want other protection? Her delicate frame will sink beneath the fatigue of wandering through the forest. Perhaps she may—

Mar. Hark! I hear footsteps! Should it be our enemies—Let us instantly conceal ourselves! [*They retire up*, L.]

Re-enter THEODORE, R.

The. I am quite spent and faint. I could soon have mastered one; but when they all set upon me, I was fain to take to my heels, and no disgrace either: no man is obliged to fight against odds.

Ray. [*Coming forward.*] Can it be? Theodore, have you not seen the Lady Agnes?

The. What, my master! St. Dennis be praised! Now I fear them not, if there are fifty of them. Follow me instantly, signor: the three villains whom we met at the cottage in the forest have just forced the Lady Agnes from me, and confined her in a cave not far distant.

Ray. Ha!—Wait you here, Marguerette; we will hasten and effect her rescue, or perish in the attempt.

Mar. No, signor; I will accompany you. I know every nook and turn in the cave, and may, perhaps, render you some service.

The. This way, then—follow me! [*Exeunt*, R. U. E.]

SCENE VII.—*The Interior of the Robber's Cave.*

AGNES *discovered chained to a rock*, R.—ROBERT, JAQUES, *and* CLAUDE, *seated at a table*, C.

Claude. Nay, you need not blame me; it was not fault of mine.

Jaq. Of what consequence is the fellow's escape?

Rob. The utmost. My revenge is never to be gratified. He fought like a devil! Had I been no more fatigued than you were, I would have followed him to the verge of the forest, ere he should have escaped me.

Jaq. Come, a truce with reproaches. Here's one cup to our better success in future!

Claude. With all my heart; and, for the present, let us lay by our arms. [*They rise, place their pistols on the table, and come forward.*]

Jaq. How shall we dispose of the prize we have already secured?

Rob. I have thought of that. We want a housekeeper to supply the place of Marguerette: she shall be the wife of one of us—let her take her choice; and, if it is not her own fault, she may be as happy as an empress.

Claude. Excellent! You hear, lady, what we have determined: which of us do you choose to have for a husband?

Jaq. Look at us; we are three stout, well-made fellows;—you might make a worse choice, my dear, even if you had a hundred to pick from.

Rob. You see we use no compulsion. Take your choice. Speak: for which of us do you decide?

Agnes. For neither!—Death would be more welcome!

Rob. This scorn, lady, will be of no avail. Recollect that you are entirely in our power: if you refuse our love, you may perhaps feel our vengeance.

Agnes. Be it so!—I would welcome the blow which freed me from your importunities.

Jaq. Entreat her no more; she is in our power, and must yield. Here are dice: we will throw and see who is to have her; and let the others quietly resign her to the winner.

Rob. It shall be so. Now fortune favour the brave!—[*They throw the dice.*] The chance is mine! [*Unfastening Agnes' chain.*] And thus I take possession of my bride!

Agnes. If you possess one spark of humanity, I implore you to restore me to my friends;—believe me, you will be rewarded even beyond your wishes; and I will pledge my word that no measures shall be taken to deprive you of liberty.

Rob. Rely upon it, that unless you can a second time elude our vigilance, you will never again behold other friends than those who now stand before you. Recollect, you are destined to be my wife.

Agnes. Thy wife!—I will perish first!

Rob. I may find a way to lower your tone, my haughty lady. I am absolute here; therefore, dread to disobey me.

Agnes. Monster! I neither fear thy power nor thy threats! Think'st thou that Agnes will ever join herself with a villain and a murderer—a wretch, whose hands are dyed with the blood of innocents? No! rather than consent, let me be the next victim of your cruelty!

Rob. Be't so! [*Aiming a dagger at her.*] Take, then, the reward of thy insolence!

Agnes. [*Screaming.*] Oh! [*She avoids the blow, and kneels.*]

MUSIC.—*Enter* RAYMOND, THEODORE, *and* MARGUERETTE, *rushing in hastily,* L.—*Raymond attacks Robert, who falls wounded; and as he rises, and aims a blow at Raymond, Marguerette snatches a pistol from his belt, and shoots him—Agnes rises—Theodore darts furiously on Claude, and overcomes him—Jaques is shot by Agnes with a pistol dropped by Claude.—Raymond and Agnes meet—they embrace, and kneel,* C.—*a loud crash is heard—the back of the cavern falls to pieces, and discovers the* BLEEDING NUN, *in a blue ethereal flame, invoking a blessing upon them—she slowly ascends, still blessing them—they form a tableau, and the curtain descends.*

DISPOSITION OF THE CHARACTERS AT THE FALL OF THE CURTAIN.

THE BLEEDING NUN.

RAYMOND. AGNES.

ROBERT. JAQUES

CLAUDE. MAR. THEO.

THE END.

ADVERTISEMENT

THIS Play is avowedly founded on the Romance of the MONK. *The Author enters not into the discussion which that work has produced.*[1] *His attempt has been to dramatise the leading incident of the Romance, without recourse to the supernatural agency. Happy shall he feel, if what he has done be thought not to discredit a production, of which the interest has never been exceeded. For difference of opinion he is fully prepared:-but the generous approbation of the* AUTHOR OF THE ROMANCE *might console him under any objections from the uncandid;-those of Genius and Judgment it is becoming to bear with fortitude and respect.*

To the acting of Mr. KEMBLE *the Author has so great obligation, that it would be a treason against excellence not to leave his sense of it upon record. He has many acknowledgments to make to his* OTHER FRIENDS, *for doing much, where he knows himself to have done less.*

1 A reference to the controversy surrounding *The Monk's* supposed immorality and blasphemy.

THE CHARACTERS

Aurelio . . . . Mr. KEMBLE
Raymond . . . . Mr. BARRYMORE
Lorenzo . . . . Mr. C. KEMBLE
Christoval . . . . . . Mr. BANNISTER, Jun.
Zingaro . . . . Mr. ARCHER
Hilario . . . . Mr. MADDOCKS
Bonaventure . . . . Mr. SPARKS
Pedro . . . . Mr. WEWITZER
Juan . . . . Mr. WENTWORTH
Claude . . . . Mr. WEBB
Lopez . . . . Mr. EVANS
Servant . . . . Mr. RYDER

Miranda (Eugenio) . . . . . Mrs. SIDDONS
Agnes . . . . Mrs. POWELL
St. Agatha . . . . Miss TIDSWELL
Teresa . . . . Miss WENTWORTH
Zingarella . . . . Mrs. BLAND
Antonia . . . . Miss HEARD
Leonella . . . . Mrs. SPARKS

Monks, Nuns, Gypsies, Soldiers, &c.

SCENE-MADRID.

AURELIO AND MIRANDA

ACT I.

SCENE I.-*The Cathedral Church of Madrid.*
A number of persons going out from the service.

LORENZO *and* CHRISTOVAL *come forward.*

Lor. Well, Christoval, you see your sister Miranda is not in the church.

Chris. No; but I am, and that's equally strange. I have told you of her sudden manner of quitting home?

Lor. Yes, and it is no slight instance of the ardor with which that sex pursues its object, whatever it be.

Chris. She was upon a visit at the Countess Osorio's seat, when she first heard this Aurelio preach: and the last intelligence I had of her was, that since her return to Madrid she was here morning, noon, and night, whenever there was a chance of hearing him.

Lor. I must confess, I half excuse Miranda. In spite of the lovely object who sat opposite, there were times when his eloquence drew me so irresistibly, that beauty could only divide the hour with him.

Chris. He awes me by his manner, I think-the severity of his eye, the loftiness of his carriage, the authority of his voice.

Lor. Nay, let us do him justice. His piety is unaffectedly grand, and his learning profound; and his command over the passions instantaneous and absolute.

Chris. I only wish the truant Miranda was here to complete this eulogium. My life on't, she would discover the grace and beauty of his person, which you have omitted-the more striking to women, as, from his order, they can cherish no hope. O, nothing is so precious to a female as what's unattainable. But who are these?

Lor. Ha! why the young one is the sweetest creature in the universe; the very enchantress that bewitched me just now. I'll accost her. Do you amuse the old woman, while I endeavor to get from her, who, and what she is.

Chris. And so, I must make the old hen cluck, while you inveigle the young pullet![1]

Lor. What! not in friendship, Don?

Chris. Well, well-you know that way I'm your slave.

Enter ANTONIA *and* LEONELLA.

[*They approach them ceremoniously.*]

Lor. Well, Signora, what do you think of our renowned Preacher? the triumphant Orator! the Man of Holiness as he is styled!

Ant. He surpasses all my expectations. His eloquence sunk deeply in my heart. The very sound of his voice affected me in a manner I cannot describe-though never heard it before, it did not seem strange to me-it pierced my very soul, and commanded my affection as well as reverence.

Lor. What think you of his countenance?

1 *pullet*: a young hen from the time she begins to lay till the first moult, after which she is a full-grown hen or fowl (OED).

Ant. It is of the first order of manly beauty: yet the searching severity of his eye, whilst it announces the keenness of his scrutiny, warns you of the terror of his rebuke. His is the front of purity, and vice must be abash'd before it.

Lor. See! He is returning to his monastery.

[*The organ plays a fugue, while* Aurelio, *preceded by boys with incense, and followed by the Fathers of his Monastery, walks from the top of the stage down, and quits the cathedral, making signs of his benediction upon the people.*]

Leon. Well, for my part, I wonder what can make people take such delight in gazing after him! Mercy upon me, I did but give a peep up, as it were, at his face, and he frowned so sternly upon me, that I tremble every joint of me.

Chris. O, 'tis very distressing indeed, to be measured in that way by a large bright, black, piercing eye, reading all that we meant should lie hidden in the bottom of that sacred well, one's own conscience.

Ant. With what humility, yet, at the same time, with what dignity did he retire from our admiring veneration.

Leon. Dignity! Why he is doubtless a person of quality.

Chris. Ah, Signora, one may see how thoroughly you observe mankind! What wisdom! what experience, you manifest!

Leon. O, Saint Barbara! You are too polite, Signor. [Christoval *draws* Leonella *a little aside.*]

Lor. Without absolutely saying so, the chance, I confess, is, that he had no noble origin. Report says, that, while a child, he was observed by some of the Monks among a gang of gypsies, who begged constantly at the Abbey-gates, and who, noticing his quick parts,[1] took him into the Monastery-there, at the proper age, he made his profession.

Ant. What is mentioned of his conduct?

Lor. That his mortification[2] and penance have been extreme. Sensible of no imperfections in himself, his severity to others is unbounded. This would be thought blameable; but he tempers the austerity of his religion with so much generosity of sentiment, his charity is so large, and his judgment so enlightened, that he is become the idol, as well as the wonder of all ranks throughout Madrid.

Ant. I regret that my retirement in Murcia kept me so long from the knowledge of your city's chief ornament.

Lor. Do you intend to stay long here? If you will allow myself, (Don Lorenzo) or Don Christoval, my friend, to use our influence for your service, I believe you will find that the attention we shall be proud of may not be unworthy of your acceptance.

[Christoval *and* Leonella *advance.*]

Leon. Never tell me, Signor. His time is not yet come. Averse to the sex! Let me see such a man insensible to charms he might meet with! Let me find beauty in tears (and that's always irresistible) confessing at his feet, (for Heaven knows we have all of us some peccadillos upon our consciences,) and then, what becomes of his apathy?

---

1 *quick parts*: a reference to Ambrosio's sharp mind.
2 *mortification*: the subjection or bringing under control of one's appetites and passions by the practice of austere living, esp. by the self-infliction or voluntary toleration of bodily pain or discomfort (OED).

Chris. Why indeed, Madam, if you were thus before him:-

Leon. I vow, Signor Cavalier, you are the politest, finest gentleman! [*They retire.*]

[Antonia *and* Lorenzo *advance.*]

Ant. I know not why I should resist your curiosity, and, though a stranger to me, I feel no repugnance to gratify it. I am the niece of the late Duke of Medina. My birth cost my mother her life. My father did not long survive her. The Duke, my uncle, received us: but he is lately dead too; and a very distant branch of the family has succeeded to the title and domains. Upon coming to take possession, he unfeelingly cast us out, with no other means, than what the few jewels I could call my own might produce. O, had my brother lived!-

Leon. Yes, Signor, she tells you truth. The dear child's dependance is now solely upon me,-unless his Majesty is graciously pleased to order the selfish Don Pedro to make her a suitable allowance,[1] or, if that cannot be done, render her indebted for independance to his own royal bounty.

Chris. How long has your brother been dead?

Ant. I never knew him:-he died ere I was born-at least he died to us-for in his infancy he was lost; and all the search that could be made was ineffectual-nor have the faintest tidings of him reach'd us since.

Lor. May I hope you will allow me to second your application to the King?-My family is possess'd of some influence.-Permit me to wait upon you where I may learn more fully-

1 *suitable allowance*: in other words, enough money to cover Antonia's living expenses.

Ant. That I must absolutely forbid. As you would retain my favourable opinion, here we must take leave.

Leon. [*to Chris.*] Well, I will not refuse my hand. [Chris. *kissess her hand, and* Leon. *and* Ant. *exeunt.*]

Lor. Loveliest of your sex, farewell!

Chris. Don Lorenzo!

Lor. What say'st thou, Christoval?

Chris. I beseech you provide yourself with a new friend. Flesh and blood can't bear the service you put me upon. I am going to the druggist's.

Lor. Why, man, why?

Chris. To buy hemony, to be sure. A full pound of myrrh, cinnamon, and aloes, would not sweeten my imagination.[2]

Lor. Her eyes did seem two stars new shot from heav'n.
The messengers of blessedness to man!

Chris. Nay, we had eyes that shot too, and very furiously. Their squint kept me up a kind of a cross-fire, like the two salient angles of a bastion;[3] 'twas death to come between 'em.

Enter RAYMOND.

Lor. Don Christoval, look yonder at that man,
Close-muffed in his cloak-just by the pillar.
He's lurking for some mischief here, I doubt.

2 *hemony* (variation of *hæmony*): From Milton's *Comus*, an imaginary plant having supernatural virtues (OED); *myrrh*: A bitter, aromatic gum resin exuded by various Arabian and African trees. Used in perfumes and as an ingredient of incense (OED).
3 *salient angles of a bastion*: the angles pointing away from the center of a fortification (OED).

Chris. I'm sure of it. Ah! well-said, Signor Shadow!
See, how he drops a letter at the foot
Of old cold stone St. Francis, hard as marble
Can make him 'gainst a lover's rhapsodies.

Lor. And now he plants himself behind the column,
To watch th'event. But look, what's this approaching?

Chris. The fine old hen St. Clare, and all her chickens-Some of 'em game; my life upon it.

Enter the PRIORESS *followed by* NUNS.

CHORUS.

"Mark! how the sacred calm, that breathes around,

Bids every fierce tumultuous passion cease!"

[Agnes, *in the procession, drops her rosary at the foot of the Statue; and stooping takes up the letter.*]

Lor. By hell, my sister Agnes. [Raymond *goes out satisfied.*]

Nay, nay, my Spaniard, you shall not escape me. [*Rushes after with* Christoval.]

[*The second stanza of the Chorus taken up by the Nuns. The procession moves on, and the scene closes as they are singing.*]

CHORUS.

"In still small accents whispering from the ground

A grateful earnest of eternal peace." [*Exeunt.*]

SCENE II.-*A Street before the Cathedral.*

RAYMOND *enters hastily, followed by* LORENZO *and* CHRISTOVAL.

Lor. Stay, Signor Lurker!
And tell me what clandestine correspondence
You carry on with this chaste sisterhood?

Ray. That voice! Lorenzo, is it you, my friend?
Well met-I could not hope for this encounter;
Yet willingly refer me to your justice.
Say, is not that Don Christoval?

Chris. The same. Come here in search of my sister Miranda. I could have wish'd myself better employment, than hunting after a capricious woman.

Ray. Lorenzo, you are prepossess'd, I see.
Go to my lodgings: there I will detail,
As truly as I do my sins to Heav'n,
All that has pass'd between me and your sister.

Lor. Take heed, Don Raymond! By my life I swear,
If any indirect and treacherous means
Have warp'd my sister Agnes from her duty,-

Ray. You shall behold my very secret soul;
And must be satisified.

Chris. We will be satisfied.

Lor. Come then.-Don Raymond!-but you shall have hearing.
[*Exeunt.*]

SCENE III.-*The Cell of* AURELIO.

Enter AURELIO-*the Fathers* HILARIO *and* BONAVENTURE *attending him.*

Aur. Brethren, I thank you. Yet, while lowly bending
For courtesy so gratifying,-let me
Be just to your most exemplary virtues:-
Under the fost'ring dew of holiness,
If I have yielded worthy fruits of piety,
Be all the praise to you, and to your order.

Hil. We bless the hour, when the especial love
Of favouring Heaven gave you to our charge.

Bon. Be yours the glory, that we boast a man
Whom vice could never warp.

Hil. Be all your meditations, visions, pray'rs,
Propitious as your eloquence. [*Exeunt Monks.*]

Aur. Farewell.
Yes, here indeed I triumph! here indulge
The pride of mastering the human mind.
It *is* my pride, to write upon the heart
The words of truth in characters of fire.
O sacred pledge of unpolluted life!
Earnest, that abstinence from vain delights,
Passions subdu'd and sacrific'd to duty,
Are sanctify'd, and minister to Heav'n.
And yet-am I indeed secure from frailty?
A man-whose very nature leads to error:
Here, in retirement, that I liv'd unstain'd
Is scarce a wonder.-Summon'd to the world,

Courted by wealth and power, and wit, and-beauty,-
How will Aurelio stand the tempting siege?
May not the mounds of abstinence give way,
And nature's passions, like a flood, o'erwhelm me? [*A knocking heard.*]
Who knocks there?

[Eugenio *without.*]

Eug. 'Tis Eugenio.

Aur. Enter, fon.

Enter EUGENIO, *with a basket of flowers.*

Eug. Most holy Father, pardon this intrusion.
I have a friend lies dangerously sick,
And would entreat your pray'rs in his behalf.
To piety like yours Heav'n will be bounteous.

Aur. I will remember him at morn and eve,
And in the solemn hour, when midnight calls
The brotherhood to their most awful duties,
Your poor sick friend shall never be forgotten.
What have you in your basket, kind Eugenio?

Eug. Some of those flow'rs, which most, I think, you love.
Let me arrange them, Father, in your cell. [*He does so.*]

Aur. There's something strangely winning in this boy:
These simple acts of friendship from him charm me.
Great benefits flow rarely through the world:
But calm attentions, like a gentle wind,
Waft our frail vessel down the stream of time,
In one unruffled, even, steady voyage,
Till we are harbour'd in eternity.

[*To* Eugenio.] I saw you not at church this morning, son.

Eug. Yet I was present, Father. Grateful as I am
For your protection, counsel, nay esteem,
Ah! could I fail, to witness all your triumph?

Aur. My triumph! O, my son, how vain a thought!
The pow'r was Heav'n's-to Heav'n be all the glory!-
Then you were satisfied with my discourse?

Eug. How say you, satisfy'd! O never heard I
Such eloquence, save once-save only once.

Aur. When was that once, Eugenio?

Eug. When you preach'd
On the late Abbot's sudden malady.

Aur. And were you present when I knew you not?

Eug. Ah! had I perish'd, ere I saw that day,
What endless sufferings had my youth escap'd!

Aur. How! Sufferings at your age, my son!

Eug. Yes, sufferings,
Which known would raise your anger and your pity-
The torment and the transport of my being.
Yet here I hop'd my bosom would feel tranquil,
But apprehension tortures me ev'n here.
O God, how wretched is a life of fear!
In the noviciate I have enter'd on
I've giv'n up all the world, and its delights;
Your friendship is the only blessing left me.
If I lose that-O, if I lose that, Father,
I tremble for th' effects of my despair.

Aur. You apprehend the loss of my esteem!
Be comforted; it is no transient sentiment,
Lightly bestowed, capriciously resum'd,
'Tis merit only claims, and will preserve it.
But for your suff'rings, let that friendship teach you,
To trust me with their cause, and if relief
Be in my power-

Eug. 'Tis in no power but yours.
Yet, ah! you must not know them-Did I dare
Avow them to you, you would hate and loath me,
Drive me with ignominy from your sight,
And give me to the scorn of all mankind.

Aur. Impossible, my son. Let me entreat you.

Eug. I cannot-dare not-Ah, enquire no further! [*Exit in great emotion.*]

Aur. [*after a pause.*] Mysterious youth! Within two little months
How deeply is he rooted in my heart!
His voice affects me ev'n to melancholy!
His manners are the gentlest sure on earth!
As far as his retiring modesty
Allows the eye to note his lineaments,
His features seem of female loveliness! [*Bell rings.*]
But hark!-I must prepare me to attend
The Sisters of St. Clare in the Confessional.-
That duty done, my dearest care will be
To win the confidence of this poor boy,
And heal, or share, the sorrows of his breast. [*Exit.*]

ACT II.

SCENE I.-*The Convent.*

AURELIO *sitting in the Confessional Chair.* AGNES *kneeling, as at Confession.*

Aur. Arise, my daughter, purified from error.
Offences light as these find easy pardon.
[Agnes *in rising drops a letter from her bosom. It falls at the Abbot's feet.*]
Stay, Agnes, you have dropt a paper.

Agn. Ah! [*Turns suddenly round, and flies to regain it.*]

Aur. Hold! I must read this letter.

Agn. Then I'm lost.

Aur. [*Reads*]. "Dearest Agnes, all is ready for your escape. I tremble every moment lest your situation be observ'd by your companions. Immediate flight can alone save you from shame and punishment. At the garden door, to-night by twelve, I will be ready to receive you."
This letter, girl, must to the Prioress. [*Going.*]

Agn. Yet I conjure you, stay. O holy Sir,
With pity view the error of my youth;
Conceal the guilty weakness of a wretch!
Here, at your feet, and bathing them with tears,
I supplicate for mercy. Hide my fault;
Let not the hand of scorn write shame upon me.
And here I vow, be angels witness for me,
To pass my rest of life in expiation.

Aur. Amazing confidence! Shall folly stain
The virgin-tended altar of St. Clare?
And shall we cherish foul incontinence?

Agn. O treat me not so harshly. Think, I charge you,
Of that oppression, which a daughter suffers,
When buried by her parents from the world,
From social joy, from friendship, and from love!
O shield my character from infamy;
Restore my soul to virtue and to Heav'n!

Aur. You have profan'd the sacred veil; and can you
Conceive yourself entitled to forgiveness?
I must have way. Where is the Prioress?

Agn. Deem me not harden'd in unseemly passion.
Long ere compulsion forc'd me to these walls,
The partner of my fault possess'd my heart.
Accident only let me know he liv'd.
Could I refuse to meet whom I ador'd?
Till often mingling tears and stol'n embraces,
Caution was lost-he press'd, and ruin found me.
Feel for my state, about to be a mother;
Restore the letter! Save me from destruction!

Aur. This is to add audacity to guilt.
Mother, St. Agatha, I say. [*She catches his robe.*]

Agn. O Father,
Think of the innocent I nourish in me,
Living, unconscious of my agony.
O, do not lay its nursery in the dust,
And make its cradle in its mother's grave!

Aur. I must not hear you. Where's the Prioress?

Agn. O cruel, cruel-Mercy! Heav'n sustain me! [*She sinks to the ground.*]

Enter the PRIORESS *and* NUNS.

Aur. How shall I speak?-Peruse that impious letter,
Dropt by the Sister Agnes at confession.

Agn. [*Starting up.*] Hear me, thou man of sternness, hard, obdurate!
You could have sav'd my honour from contempt,
Have giv'n my days to peace and penitence.
Arrogant confidence in your own strength
Makes you reject the contrite sinner's prayer,
Makes you disdain a mother's agonies,
And therefore on your conscience and your soul
I lay the death of me and of my child.

Aur. Forbear these ravings-Sisters, take her hence! [*They seize her.*]

Agn. No: in the pangs of death I would be heard. [*She bursts from them.*]
What trials has your boasted virtue vanquish'd?
You fled them, like a coward, unattempted.
But mark! the hour of proof must come to all!
If in that hour you feel, that man is weak;
While shudd'ring you look back on your own crimes,
O then remember Agnes and her faults!
May yours compar'd plant horror in your heart!
Remember Agnes then,-nor hope for mercy,
But die the frantic victim of despair.

Aur. Haste to the convent with her-Let her penance
Be strict; and striking terror by its nature!
Should guilt like this experience mitigation,

The place of holiness will be a seat
For loath'd intemperance.-Away with her.

Agn. O grant me, Heav'n, the mercy they deny me. [*Exeunt.*]

SCENE II.[1]-*The Garden of* AURELIO'*s Monastery.*

A rustic Hermitage on one side. The Abbey in the distance.

Enter EUGENIO.

Eug. O miserable state, wretched Miranda!
O fruitless stratagem! Was it for this
I left friends, fortune, family, and honour?
My irresistible and fatal love
Will force its way through all this vain disguise.
Yet how reveal it to him?-How support
The lightnings of his anger?-My weak spirits
Shrink from the thought, and my chill'd heart dies in me.
[*Sinks down upon the seat in dejection.*]

AURELIO *enters unseeing and unseen.*

Aur. However painful, I have executed
The task impos'd upon me by my office.
Penance and meditation may perhaps
Preserve the fallen Agnes from perdition.
I've done my duty! Why then do I feel
As if my conduct merited reproach,
As though beyond the size of the offence?
Would I could banish this solicitude!
In this sequester'd spot I may regain

1 In Bell's printing of the play, this and most subsequent scenes are simply labeled "SCENE." I have added numbering to allow for easier reference.

My wonted firmness and tranquillity. [*Seeing* Eugenio, *he draws back.*]

Eug. [*Surveying the inscriptions.*] My heart refuses to admit the truth.
No: Solitude supplies no balm to me.
O could I feel disgust at all mankind;
Did scorn, injustice, treachery, combine
To plant the sullen fiend Misanthropy
Within this breast, how happy might I be!

Aur. Seek in misanthropy for happiness!
That's a strange thought, Eugenio, pardon me.
One so young too to wish for solitude,
And animate its bower with hate alone!

Eug. 'Twas a vain wish, I own, most holy Father,
Yet gives my only hope of earthly comfort.

Aur. Alas, Eugenio, churlish solitude
Is seldom the abode of peace or virtue.
While rankling hate inflames the mental wound,
The wretch who flies from men may think him happy;
May bless the hour, that tore him from the scene
Of broken hopes and violated vows.
But time still dries the tear on sorrow's cheek,
And injuries forgot are half aton'd

Eug. Yet tell me, Father, when his worldly pangs
Corrode and vex his chasten'd heart no more,
Then does not virtue smile upon his bower,
And fold him in her friendly arms to rest?

Aur. No! These are visions of the social man.
The hermit views a melancholy waste
Where'er he strays; pores on the setting sun
With vacant eyes; and when the falling dews
Drive him from gloomy, fruitless contemplation,
His cell is void of all the joys of home:
His lonely meal nor satisfies nor cheers:
But on his sinking heart sits blank despair,
Bids him forsake the tasteless food he loaths,
And be a solitary wretch no longer.

Eug. O that I ne'er had seen this Abbey's walls!

Aur. Eugenio, whence this change, my tender friend?
What! can you wish that you had never known me?

Eug. You, you! Ah no-Yet, Father, pity me!
Indulge this loneliness! The crowded world
Can give none willing to partake my sorrows.

Aur. At least confide them to my friendly trust;
And if my aid, my pity can alleviate-

Eug. Yours only can. And oh! how willingly
Would I reveal my heavy hoard of anguish,
But that I fear-

Aur. What should you fear, my son?

Eug. My weakness known would lose me your esteem;
You would abhor me for the confidence.

Aur. Abhor you! No-It is not in my power!
You give the greatest pleasure to my life:
Reveal then your affliction, while I swear-

Eug. Yes, swear, that, be my secret what it may,
You will not force me to forsake the Abbey.

Aur. I promise it, my friend, by all that's holy.
And now explain, and trust to my indulgence.

Eug. Hear then with pity, hear, rever'd Aurelio,
And call up ev'ry latent weakness in you,
To aid that pity, while my desperate passion
Bids me confess your suppliant is-Miranda! [*Throws back her cowl.*]

Aur. [*after a pause.*] Begone, or let me leave you.

Mir. Stay, I charge you.
Heav'n ne'er inspir'd a purer flame than mine.
Listen in mercy!

Aur. Can you nourish hope
I may permit your residence with me?
Ha! whence these tumults beating in my heart? [*Aside.*]
Think of the violation of my order!
Nor dare I yield myself to such temptation.

Mir. O listen to me, most ador'd Aurelio!
Grant me the blessing only to be near you:
Keep my sex secret: nay, forget it quite;
For my affection-hear me!-is so pure,
So far sublim'd from ev'ry frailer thought,
That seraphs burn not with a holier fire.

Aur. To-morrow you must leave the Monastery.

Mir. And will you banish your poor friend for ever?
And will you drive her out a wanderer?
Rend the poor heart that only beats for you,

And spurn me to an undeserved grave?
O do not, my Aurelio!

Aur. Sweet Miranda,
I pity you-but am not to be mov'd.
To-morrow you must leave these walls for ever. [*Going.*]

Mir. Did you not swear?-

Aur. You know my resolution.
You sue in vain.

Mir. Go then, barbarian, go.
But this resource you cannot rob me of. [*Draws a dagger.*]
Shall I endure the keen reproach of friends,
The vulgar scoff, or, what is worse, the pity?
No: never will I quit these walls alive.

Aur. Hold, hold-most lovely, most unhappy woman!

Mir. You are determined, Father: so am I.
The moment that you leave me, here I swear
To finish life and misery together.
Or your lov'd hand shall lead me on to joy-
Or my sure means conduct me to perdition.

Aur. Stay; thou delightful, beauteous mischief-stay!
Yes, stay Miranda, though for my destruction! [*Exit.*]

Mir. My heav'n is won. My triumph is complete:
Love lights his torch of bliss, and burns in rapture. [*Exit.*]

SCENE III.-*The Garden Gate of the Convent.*

The PRIORESS *and Sister* TERESA.

Prio. The hour draws on. How left you the weak, wicked one?

Ter. In agony so violent, as to produce the infant witness of her guilt.

Prio. Holy St. Clare! I who have passed my life in a most mortifying denial, to build my Convent a reputation, to be sham'd at these years-and before Aurelio too, of all the world-the man whose praise would make the fortune of any Domina in Spain!

Ter. Has my holy mother determin'd on her punishment?

Prio. 'Tis likely her extremity may spare me that talk-If she recovers, woe be to the harlot! In the mean time, Teresa, let no one have access to her cell. Give out she died this evening.

Ter. Yet consider: She is of a noble family. Do you think no search will be made what becomes of her? If they credit her death, will they not expect her funeral to be public?

Prio. Doubtless: that can be easily arranged. You shall be acquainted with all my plan ere we retire to rest. Now seek out Pedro, the gardener, and give him instructions what he must answer to any enquiry. I'll again to Agnes. [*Exit.*]

Ter. Pedro, where are you? Pedro I say. O here he comes.

Enter PEDRO.

Pedro. Here, here, my sweet saint. What commands have you for Pedro? By St. Anthony, my afternoon devotion has stretched plaguily into evening service. Your Malaga is a very dry wine. I'm rather dry myself-It suits my palate exactly.

Ter. Pedro, our lady has detected a most shameless piece of villainy.

Pedro. [*Aside.*] O Lord, what's in the wind now? I'm sober in a moment.

Ter. The Sister Agnes-

Pedro. [*Aside.*] Pray heaven they don't suspect me to be in the plot!

Ter. Has been detected in an amour.

Pedro. [*Aside.*] Yes, and I shall be detected too, if I don't get her off.

Ter. The appointment to go off with her betrayer this night has fallen into our hands.

Pedro. [*Aside.*] Don Raymond will be here in a moment,-and then I'm ruined.

Ter. In her condition, no wonder at the effect of such a discovery! She expired in child-birth this evening.

Pedro. Sweet creature! [*Aside.*] O, don't mention such shocking offences to me. [*Pushing her off.*]

Ter. If any enquiry should be made after her, you now know what to answer. [*Exit.*]

Pedro. Aye, aye. Detected, dead, her infant too perhaps! How shall I meet Don Raymond? how stab him to the heart, when it beats high with the hope of clasping in his arms all that is dearest to him? Poor gentleman! By Teresa's silence on that head, they don't know him.-O, if they find him out, their fury at the disgrace of the Convent will send him speedily to the Inquisition. Thank Heaven, they don't suspect me! If they did, they might torture me, but they should never make me treacherous. It's about time. I'll see that they have actually retired. [*Enters the garden.*]

Enter RAYMOND *and* LORENZO.

Ray. I wonder Pedro is not here on guard.
If his attendance now should be prevented,
We have the cords, and scale the garden walls.

Lor. It wants a trifle only of the hour.

PEDRO *returns.*

Pedro. They are retired. All's safe. The gates are clos'd.
O yonder sure they are. I'll give the word.
But how reveal the tale? [*Aloud.*] "'Tis almost twelve."

Ray. He gives the word! How my heart dances in me!
Pedro, my friend-Where is my beauteous Agnes?
Is she not ready? Nothing has occurr'd
To stop her flight!

Pedro. Who is that with you, Signor?

Ray. My noble friend her brother, whose full heart
O'erflows with fondness for her: and he comes
To end captivity and doubt together,
To give her to her Raymond. Why this shyness?
Come forth, my Agnes, now while none observe us.

Lor. [*advances*] Yes, my dear sister-'Tis Lorenzo's self,
That breaks the galling fetters of your bondage,
And gives you freely to the man you love.

Pedro. I cannot speak to him-my heart is stifled.
The poor, dear lady!

Ray. Pedro, speak, what mean you?
Why are you dumb? What mean your hands thus clasp'd,
Your bended eyes, that seem to penetrate
The very earth rather than look on me?
Is not my Agnes safe? Are we discover'd?

Pedro. All that you fear is true. I cannot speak it;
Nor is it fit abrupt to strike your sense
With tidings that would murder as they fell.

Ray. Yet tell me all. She is detected!-Well-
I can bear that-We'll heal that trivial wound;
No scar of shame shall mark it to the world!
But she is well.

Pedro. [*to Lorenzeo, drawing him aside.*] I am not man enough.
Tell him,-(You are a scholar, and will wisely;
You are her brother, therefore will with feeling;)
Tell him her agony at the detection
Brought on the crisis of a mother's pains,
And in the conflict she and all are lost. [*Exit in great emotion.*]

Ray. The news that's fitter for a brother's ear
Than for a lover's, tells itself, untold.
Then she is dead? Your silence, my Lorenzo,
Is both my answer and my condemnation!
Reproaches me for a dear sister's death,
And barbs the arrow conscience fixes here.
Sweet innocent! 'tis I, whose selfish love
Brought shame and death upon thee. Cursed Raymond
Alone could blast the promise of thy life!

Lor. I cannot give thee what I want myself-
Besides, what comfort lies in words?-She's dead!
And you must mourn her loss as her adorer,
I as her brother-
Let us from this place!
And keep yourself conceal'd-You know the peril
That would attend on your discovery!-
My firmness staggers under this rude shock;
And calls for lonely thought, to nerve my mind!
Come, my more wretched friend! My brother, come.
[*Leads him off.*]

ACT III.

SCENE I.-LEONELLA's *House.*

Enter LEONELLA *and* ANTONIA.

Leon. Well, Niece, nothing of your professing Lorenzo! So passionate a lover, and so dilatory in his visits; but his coming at any time will make his peace. O, when I was in my teens, it was quite another affair. Such adoration! such assiduity!

Ant. There might be a difference in the manner, dear Aunt, but the passion I fancy was always nearly the same.

Leon. Oh, nothing like it, Chuck.[1] Lovers in my time were flung at such a distance-

Ant. I am afraid the distance was too great, Ma'am.

Leon. How too great, Child?

Ant. Why, ceremony kept the lovers so very far asunder, that some of the parties are never like to join issue.

Leon. Well, well, you never will become a convert to my doctrine, till you see the charming Don Christoval lead me to the altar.

Ant. I fear that altar burns only the incense, which fancy offers to the idol of Vanity.

Leon. Aye, aye. Unbelief is blind. Mark the event.

---

1 *Chuck*: A familiar term of endearment, applied to husbands, wives, children, close companions (OED).

Enter SERVANT.

Serv. A young nobleman desires the honour to kiss your hands.

Leon. Admit him. [*Exit Servant.*] My Christoval, I know it by my palpitation.

Ant. I hope it is Lorenzo. How, Don Christoval!

Enter CHRISTOVAL.

Chris. Ladies, your slave. There's my dromedary.[1] [*Aside.*]

Leon. I trust, Signor, you have enjoyed tolerable health, since I last had the honour of your attendance.

Chris. Never better in my whole existence.

Leon. Nay, nay, not quite so well, I am sure. Absence must chill the lover's heart; nor can its purple streams e'er bound with joy, till she for whom it beats restore their vital heat.

Chris. Where the devil is this Lorenzo? I shall be ravished if he does not come to my rescue. ('Sblood,[2] I'd sooner lay me in the sear-cloth[3] with an Egyptian mummy, than come within the clasp of that hyæna.) [*Aside.*]

Ant. Poor woman! how ridiculous she makes herself. I must step in to his relief. [*Aside.*] -Signor Don Christoval, when did you last see your friend Lorenzo?

---

1 *dromedary*: A stupid, bungling fellow (OED). Christoval is mocking his own behavior.

2 *'sblood*: A euphemistic shortening of *God's blood*, used as an oath (OED)

3 *sear-cloth* (variation of *cerecloth*): used for wrapping a dead body in; a waxed winding-sheet or a winding-sheet in general (OED).

Chris. Heaven bless you, Madam! He directed me to meet him here. The last time we parted, I left him robbing the church!

Ant. Robbing the church!

Chris. Yes, Madam, of a Sister.

Ant. How, Sir! [*alarmed*] Are you in earnest, Signor?

Leon. To be sure he is, Child. O, the difference of men!

Chris. Yes, yes-But it is his own sister.

Ant. Oh!-I'm satisfied.

Leon. Explain yourself, Don Christoval.

Chris. The Sister Donna Agnes of St. Clare. He was about to extricate her from purgatory, and give her to the man of her heart, his friend, Don Raymond. Not finding him here, ladies, and being anxious to know his success, I humbly take my leave, and wish upon you all the felicity that your best desires could fancy, and so, ladies- [*Edging off.*]

Leon. What, and have you hired out to him all your sweet things for the day? Nothing to offer on your own account? Are all those charms which you admired so much, the ardour that you owned, the pangs you felt forgotten? Vows too poured out even at church! And was I treated only like a child-a May game-made a queen o'the May,[4] and stuck out in all the flowers of speech for a holiday foolery? [*Follows him about.*]

---

4 *queen o'the May* or *May Queen*: A girl or young woman who is chosen to preside over May Day festivities as a queen, usually being gaily dressed and crowned with flowers (OED).

Chris. Hear me, dear, good, old lady, hear me. How was it possible you should think me serious? Friendship leads a man into dreadful situations. Let me escape but this once, and if ever I am caught mumbling withered apples instead of seasonable fruit, may matrimony harpoon me! May I be bound like whalebone to the back of a grannum of eighty,[1] leave off swanskin, and warm myself with a leathern doublet![2] [*Exit.*]

Leon. O, the monster! The cruel, barbarous, perfidious, dear, handsome deluder!-But I'll forget all that. I shall go distracted with my wrongs. Such a face, that looked all sincerity! Such a tongue too, that might deceive a saint!-I feel it at my heart. O, I shall never recover it.

Ant. Come, come, Aunt-Revenge his infidelity on the whole sex. Disclaim all communion with these betrayers.

Leon. I will, Antonia. Never, though they were dying at my feet-No, not all their protestations, their despair, their death-I shall go distracted. [*Exeunt.*]

SCENE II.-AURELIO'*s Cell.*

Enter AURELIO.

Aur. In vain I strive to lull these thoughts to rest;-
Since Passion grew an inmate of my soul,
Imagination stung can rest no more.
Can Nature's impulse be unholy fire?
Yet what is virtue, but surmounted passion?

---

1 a reference to a whalebone corset on an eighty-year-old grandmother.
2 a *doublet* is a "close-fitting body-garment" (OED), so Christoval is suggesting he will wear coarse leather rather than soft swanskin flannel.

Would I had never climb'd this giddy height,
This pyramid of earthly vanity!
Each mounting step is less and less secure;
And when we reach the summit of the spire,
The very eminence disturbs the brain,
And down we fall, the scoff of humbler fools.

[MIRANDA *without.*]

Mir. Are you within, good Father?

Aur. Come in. O how that gentle voice thrills through me!

Mir. [*entering*] Are you alone, Aurelio?

Aur. Alone!-Most true!
Guilt is of dark soul, and loves privacy.

Mir. Unkind Aurelio, thus to brand as crime
A passion your own excellence inspires!

Aur. Thou dear deluder,-give me back myself.
Talk not to me of excellence and virtue,
I never had them-or, if once call'd mine,
Thy conqu'ring beauty drove them from my breast,
And fill'd it with a love I should disclaim.

Mir. When purity like yours embraces love,
It chastens it from ev'ry touch of grossness,
And makes it but the wish of soul for soul.

Aur. Enchanting accents!-but believ'd no longer.
Imperious passion scorns the frozen bounds
Of this refinement-I am new created.-
The fetters of monastic apathy
Are burst and shiver'd by resistless nature;-

The saint was all a dream-the man awakes.
How could I wish thee to forsake these walls!

Mir. What! was my very sight oppressive to thee?

Aur. Thou wonder of thy sex, in whom combine
All that can glad the eye, or charm the soul,
O, thou art born to conquer all resistance.
I see thee, angel as thou art in form,
Yet lovelier far than form alone could make thee!
Beauty is often but the painted snare
That lures the heedless eye to what is worthless-
Nature to thee has giv'n, to crown her work,
The mind, beyond the scope of vulgar being!
Intelligence she thron'd upon thy brow;
And sense and feeling do thee hourly homage.

Mir. O praise, too grateful from Aurelio's tongue,
That, like a sudden gale of rich perfumes,
Hits the frail nerves too exquisitely keen,
And pains with its delight!

Aur. 'Tis destiny.
The dreams of purity immaculate,
That virgin'd me for years, are melted all
Like the night shadows by the lord of day.
Take me, thou bright perfection, to thy arms!
Miranda, I am ever, ever thine.
[*A knocking at the door.*]
What noise was that! Retire, retire, Miranda,
Into my Oratory. Now I come. [*Exit Miranda.*]

Enter PEDRO.

What is your pleasure?

Pedro. [*Aside*] I though I saw the hem of a petticoat.-Mercy upon us! Most holy Sir, the Prioress of St. Clare would trespass on your leisure and your counsel, if for a moment only you will grant it.

Aur. I shall expect her now, so tell your lady.
I wish'd to see her.

Pedro. I will, right reverend. [*Aside*] Yes, and I'll watch you closely too. Here's a hypocrite for you! Dooms the poor Agnes to destruction for one slip, while himself riots here in security!

Aur. Art thou not gone?

Pedro. The Prioress is here.

Enter PRIORESS.

And a pitiless pair there is of ye. [*Exit.*]

Aur. May peace and blessing ever rest upon you!
How does the sister Agnes?-Well, I hope.
Poor girl! I much desir'd to speak with you,
Touching the course to win her from her error.

Prio. Her failings and her merits are with Him
Who weights us in the balance of his justice.

Aur. Most true: but something still remains with us:
I mean-to draw the sliding back to safety,
Deduce a lesson from convicted evil,
Confirm the strong, and strengthen those that tremble.

Prio. You lead me to the object of my visit.
If, holy Sir, you would but deign to treat

With eloquence like yours this foul offence,
This guilty love, that dares to profane the altar,
The lesson would be written in all hearts.

Aur. Aurelio, art thou pure thyself from stain?
Is thy robe spotless?- [*Aside.*]

Prio. Do not, Sir, deny me.
The interests of holiness are yours.

Aur. Sister, I yield with pleasure-but the subject
Seiz'd my attention on the instant hearing,
And wrapt me thus in thought.
[*A bell tolls.*]
Why tolls that bell?-

Prio. It summons us to give her to the earth.
Aur. Give her? Give whom?

Prio. I though you understood me;
The sister Agnes.

Aur. Agnes! Is she dead?
Leave me this moment-leave me, I beseech you!- [*Exit Prioress.*]
I've sacrific'd to justice, too, too sternly.

Enter MIRANDA.

O impious rigour. O inhuman pride!

Mir. Be comforted-for holy was your purpose.

Aur. Talk not to me of purposes, Miranda-
What right has man to banish pity from him?
Do we not feel we live but by its influence?

And where's infallibility in me?
Do I not find me frail and vanquish'd also?
Should Heav'n judge me, as I have judg'd poor Agnes,
What were my future portion but despair?

Mir. Let me keep peace between you and your conscience.
Her punishment was love, though dress'd in terrors.
Its rigour tended but to bring her back,
More dear to Heav'n than had she never stray'd.
Designs once pure, events must rest above.

Aur. Poor frantic wretch! Her shrieks are in my ears!
Her denunciations pierce my very brain!
"You have disdain'd to listen to compassion,
And therefore on your conscience and your soul
I lay the death of me and of my child."
Oh! thou poor lost one! all thy agonies
Are visited upon my harden'd soul,
And terribly avenge the wrongs I did thee.

Mir. 'Tis horrible. Yet hear me, Aurelio.

Aur. O come not near me. You, you make my pangs
Too keen for me to bear-For, oh! in you
I see what Agnes saw, the mind's subduer:
Conscience arous'd now tells me of my vows;
Tells me, I murder'd whom I match in guilt.
What canst thou say to dead the soul's quick nerve,
And drive away Hell's ready slave, despair?

Mir. O do not bid me leave you! Drive despair!
Yes, my Aurelio, love can chace that fiend-
It is the balm that heav'nly mercy made
To heal the wounded heart. A faithful breast

Is the soul's best physician-Trust its power..
Though in the mind the fiercest pangs increase,
Love lulls the pain, and smiles it into peace. [*Exeunt.*]

SCENE III.-*The Prado.*[1]

A gang of Gypsies enter with a fife and tabour, triangles, hand-organ,[2] *and other street music.* ZINGARELLA *suddenly stops.*

Zin. We are at our journey's end. Yonder stands the Monastery to which my father directed us. But how to gain admittance to Aurelio is the question.

Claude. What business can the tribe of Geber[3] have with his reverence, I wonder?

Zin. Listen attentively, and learn. You know how severely the late Duke de Medina persecuted our order.

Claude. Aye, aye, he filled our calendar with martyrs. The stocks, the whipping-post, and the town gaol never were so graced before.

Zin. My father resolved to take a severe revenge, and found means to steal away his nephew and heir apparent to the dukedom. The boy proved bright and apt, and the monks of that very monastery took him in, and that boy is now the famed Aurelio.

---

1 *Prado*: The proper name of the public park of Madrid, a fashionable promenade (OED).
2 *fife*: A small shrill-toned instrument of the flute kind; *tabour*: A small kind of drum; *hand-organ*: A portable barrel-organ played by means of a crank turned with the hand (OED).
3 *Geber*: variant of Guebre; an adherent of the ancient Persian religion; a Zoroastrian, fire-worshipper, Parsee (OED).

Claude. Indeed!-Aurelio!

Zin. Nothing more certain. And now we have discovered, that his sister and her aunt are come hither to solicit a pension. Lopez dogged them into the Grand Church.

Enter LOPEZ.

Lop. They are coming, they are coming. To your sleights, my dears. The young one is Antonia; the old woman, her aunt, Leonella. Strike up! and, Zingarella, prophesy.

Enter LEONELLA, ANTONIA, *and a crowd of people.*

Zin. [*Sings.*]

Cross my hand, and you shall know
All the Gypsy's art can show.
Would you have the past reveal'd,
Close by knavery conceal'd;
Would you know what blessings wait,
What ills annoy your future state;
Cross my hand, and you shall find
Destiny for once be kind.

[*The crowd gather about them.* LEONELLA *and* ANTONIA *approach.*]

Zin. [*to Antonia*] Bless you, sweet young lady! May your fate be as gentle as your countenance!

Leon. Methinks you might learn respect, good stroller.

Zin. What, to age? Then most respectfully I turn to you. Would you chose a sample of my art? Give me your hand, and be attentive. [*Sings.*]

Shrunk from splendour, let your state

Be respected, though not great.
Let not vanity engage
Your mind to trifle with your age.
All your flaunting days are over,
Never will you lure a lover:
For Ovid read some holy text;
Avoid this world, and seek the next.

Leon. O, this is an imposter, I see. Come away, child. Don't listen to her impertinence.

Zin. Art thou too an enemy to truth? Stay, I charge you. It concerns you nearly. [*Sings.*]
What a various lot is thine!
Many a strange perplexing line
Through this palm with cutting strife
Mars the quiet of thy life.
When what is deem'd your greatest loss
Is the chief champion of the cross,-
Then wealth and power consent to join
A lover's noble hand to thine.

Ant. How singular was her address to me! I would fain despise it, and yet my mind is not sufficiently strong. Is it possible that-But no, the future must be hidden from all eyes.

Leon. A saucy vermin! Avoid this world, and seek the next, indeed! I hope I am not to take a Gypsy for my ghostly director. No lover neither, when the handsomest cavalier in Spain is-O no-was dying for me at first sight!-O that my will could bring upon them all the plagues of their native Egypt!-But see, they are coming again!-Come, come. [*Exeunt.*]

CHORUS *of Gypsies.*

ACT IV.

SCENE I.

Enter RAYMOND *and* LORENZO.

Ray. My heart refuses me a place of rest!
I wander like some night-enlarged spirit,
Still loth to quit the earth, tho' all that gave
A shape, an aim, a colour to my being
Is sunk into the grave. May you be happier!

Lor. Time and my best Antonia may do much.
But my dear sister's death sits heavy on me,
And I could sink beneath my own regrets,
Did not your still superior loss arouse me,
To mitigate the sufferings of a brother.

Ray. O my Lorenzo, horrors sore besiege me.
The day-the night, are fill'd with my despair!
All day I ponder on the heav'n I lost,
And night, like a perfidious flattering foe,
Gives me again poor Agnes to my arms;
Makes me most rich in shadowy happiness,
Which the next dawning dissipates in air.

Lor. If comfort can be drawn from misery,
Calamity has fill'd your cup so full,
That you may smile at aught that threatens further.
And for these wild and feverish nightly dreams,-

Ray. Yet mark the circumstance that clothes my visions.
Last night had worn away itself in thought,
And day already dimm'd my taper's flame,

Whem slumber clos'd my eye-lids. I was led,
Methought, by some one in monkish garb,
Into an antique vault, a place of burial;
Where-side-by-side, the long-forgotten bones
Of faith's pure votaries lay fair-inscrib'd.
In the mid pathway of this ghostly hall
Sat one like sorrow's queen-Her throne the grave,
And the dull pillow on the which she lean'd,
Was a new shell of death untenanted.
The coffin-lid was off-I read its plate;
It told me that my Agnes rested there.
The seeming Monk then bade me look again:
The female form, that sat upon the ground,
Lifted her head, which till then droop'd to earth,
And call'd me by my name-But, O! that voice!-
Lorenzo, 'twas your sister's-thine, my Agnes.
While from that coffin rose a cherub shape
Bright like an angel! Beams of glory burst
From his clear flesh, and such a smile effus'd
From his soft dewy eyes that I was dazzled
And fainting with delight. "Behold thy son,"
The friendly guide exclaim'd, "thy suffering wife
Preserv'd and found, and giv'n thee from the tomb!"
I flew to clasp them; but the agony
Burst the frail thread of visionary action,
And I awoke.

Lor. Such are the shadowy trains,
Which fancy adds to double real griefs.
[*Don* CHRISTOVAL *without.*]

Chris. What ho! Where are you? Let me speak with you.

Lor. I hear Don Christoval. How ill his levity
Becomes a house like this!

Ray. Excuse me to him.
I have not yet composure fit to see him. [*Exit.*]

CHRISTOVAL *running in.*

Chris. She's alive! She's alive! Lorenzo, she lives, and I am out of breath-I can't tell you half. I should have burst my wind if it had not been for my sword-belt.-But, thank Heaven, she's alive.

Lor. Who-Who's alive?-What idle stuff is this?

Chris. Who's alive? Why, who should be? Your sister Donna Agnes-I am sure of it! I have it under her own hand! She writes me word so.

Lor. Where? How! For Heaven's sake be explicit!

Chris. I haven't the paper. No matter-I read it. It dropt upon his head.

Lor. Whose head?

Chris. Upon Pedro's, I tell you. No wonder he has been crazy ever since. [*Searches again.*] Ha! ha! 'Ecod, here it is at last-I've squeezed it into a pellet in my hand. I've lamed my fingers with clenching it.

Lor. Let me undo it, man.

Chris. No-no-You're not cool enough. [*His hand shakes so, that he is long about it: and tears the letter a little.*] There-there-Not much torn-I can read it all by heart.

Lor. O, give it me. [*Snatches the letter.*]

Chris. Ha! this is idle stuff, is it?

Enter ANTONIA.

Ant. Don Christoval, your servant!

Chris. How do you do, Sir? [*Flies to her.*] You're an angel! I'll kneel to you, I have such news-My heart's broke with joy-but she's alive.

Lor. Look here, my dear Antonia, and bless Heaven!

Ant. [*Reads.*] "Pedro, my good friend, I conjure you convey this to Don Christoval-You will hear that I am dead. My death is no doubt designed-but it has not been the consequence of my agony. AGNES."[1]

Lor. Where, where is Pedro?

Chris. He's coming as fast as possible.

Lor. And you here so long before him?

Chris. How should he come so fast as I did? My heart's twice as big. He is a friendly assistant, and only runs: Love makes me a principal, and I flew. If you should hear of any body overturned-any old woman roll'd into the kennel[2]-any chairs[3] with glass beat out of the windows, and the chairman rib-roasted with their own poles, set them all down to

1 It is unclear why Agnes would direct her letter to Don Christoval rather than her brother or lover. Equally odd is Don Christoval's exaggerated excitement upon hearing of Agnes' situation. Boaden appears to be using Don Christoval as the primary agent for expressing the overblown sentimentality of the play's conclusion.

2 *kennel*: The surface drain of a street; the gutter (OED).

3 *chair*: An enclosed chair or covered vehicle for one person, carried on poles by two men; a sedan (OED).

my account. My joy's worth a million times the damage. I'll pay it all to-morrow.

Enter PEDRO.

Here he is-Now, then, my honest delver[4]-Tell us the manner how-the place where-the time when-all this news fell upon your weak penthouse?

Pedro. Aye, aye,- [*Smiles-half-laughing, half-weeping, is unable to relate it.*]

Lor. It was in the garden, friend?

Pedro. To be sure! Oh! all the Saints!

Lor. What day was this mock funeral then performed?

Pedro. Blessed be the day I was born!

Lor. He does not understand me.

Pedro. St. Ursula, and St. Bridget! St. Agatha!-No, I blot her from the martyr-roll.

Lor. My poor, dear fellow!

Pedro. [*Falling on his knees.*] He is merciful to us all.

Chris. 'Sblood! He's bewitch'd!-Pedro.

Pedro. [*Crying.*] Aye, aye!

Chris. Zounds! the fool's in hysterics! Thus it is drink affects a soft head. The brain addles. The whole man becomes maudlin.[5] This animal now is nothing but a gross pumpkin, all water: his head is dropsical-and grief has tapp'd him.

---

4 *delver*: one who tills the ground, so in this case it is synonymous with "gardener."

5 *maudlin*: Having reached the stage of drunkenness characterized by tear-

Lor. Let him compose himself below-We'll talk to him at a fit season.

Chris. You're a pretty fellow, indeed, to travel with good news. The heart on you isn't in fault, that's the truth on't. And as for this embassy by water to our comfort, it is but an April shower-the sun-shine of the soul beams through it in the brightest colours. 'Tis Heaven's own rainbow, the sign of compassion and love. [*Leads off Pedro.*]

Lor. The difficulty now will be to deliver her from this dreadful situation.

Ant. Some management will be necessary in its disclosure to Don Raymond.

CHRISTOVAL *returning.*

Chris. I have it-I am the man for difficulties.

Lor. My dear, whimsical, faithful friend-What device is there in thy brain that thou enjoy'st so mightily?

Chris. Your sister must not be regain'd-No!-that's certain-nobody will stir in her behalf-she must be suffer'd to endure all the malignant tortures of that hell-cat. [*Walking about.*]

Lor. No!-I will make my appeal to the spiritual powers.

Chris. Heav'n help you!-you'll need it.-No, no-I'll deliver your sister-I-the maggot-pated, idle, thoughtless chough,[1] will do it. I apply to the cannon law-and rescue the captive by military ordinance-Trust to my genius, and be ready to aid me when I give the word.

---

ful sentimentality and effusive displays of affection (OED).

1 *chough*: probably a variant of *chuff*, a rustic, boor, clown, or churl (OED).

Lor. Now let us seek Don Raymond.

Chris. Be that your business. I have mightier matters.-Courage-and march. [*Exeunt.*]

SCENE II.-AURELIO'*s Cell.*

MIRANDA *enters, followed by* AURELIO.

Mir. No more-It ill become your lips to utter;
I feel myself dishonour'd to have heard
The plain avowal of illicit love.
Mark me, Aurelio: That my yielding soul
Was wholly yours, I glory to avow.
I made myself a love of character,
And bound my passion to your purity:
I knew my honour, and relied on yours.

Aur. Yet do me justice, ev'n in your displeasure.
I could not hope, and early I confess'd it,
To be allow'd to gaze upon your beauty,
Indulge the knowledge of your answ'ring love,
And not approve temptation in the grant.
I yielded my consent.

Mir. To save my life!-
Your memory is perfect, Sir-But still
Those words must come from no one but myself.

Aur. Cruel Miranda!-could you think my nature
Would e'er insult the object it adores?
If, in the hourly witness of those charms,
The fires they must excite will burst their way,
In spite of all the checks of my condition-

Mir. And what you gave in pity to my weakness,
You now would make the ruin of my fame!-
But if I thought I could be so degraded,
To fall a victim to impure desires,
I'd tear myself from thee, and all the world,
And burning shame should crumble me to ashes.

Aur. The passions Heav'n inspires his love permits.
His creatures all indulge them, and are happy.
Shall we alone disclaim the generous bliss,
And freeze the mighty fervour by caprice?

Mir. 'Tis true-the chain of love surrounds creation,
And all the various tribes of being feel it:
To man exclusively the law is giv'n,
That binds his reason and his love together,
And bids him live for one-and one alone.

Aur. Hear me protest-that you, and only you,
Shall ever reign the sovereign of my heart!-
Silence your scruples then-Accept a pledge
Sacred as if recorded at the altar.
Comply, my gracious sweetness!-Who can know it?

Mir. I shall. No, no; these solemn-sounding words
But veil the infamy that lurks beneath them,
They cannot change its colour.-Shall I speak it?
It makes of you a cheat, tho' saint without:-
And, to describe the partner of your crime,
'Tis Nature's error, an immodest woman;
A common character, but not Miranda's.

Aur. Perverse, mysterious sex!-proposing ever
Objects that mock all possible attainment.
Show them a being, who renounces love,
One covenanted to despise its power,
Him they pursue with all the rage of conquest,
And bend him to their will. The task acheiv'd
Seems to annihilate the love which prompted it,
Or fences it with scruples never dreamt on.

Mir. Thus irritated passion ever clouds
The purposes that thwart its rash indulgence.
Hear me, and weigh the motives of my conduct,
And call me then capricious or unjust.
Fatally for my peace, a slave to love,
I sought, with innocence, its safe indulgence.
I saw Aurelio awful in his virtue;-
But what repell'd the sex attracted me;
Nor could I think the highest hopes of man
Rais'd him beyond the reach of woman's love.
I did aspire to make him own a wish,
And to supply that wish by virtuous passion;
My house's power might have absolve'd his vows,
And bid his goodness blaze in social life;-
I hop'd in him a husband.

Aur. O Miranda,
Assail not thus my falt'ring resolution!
Think, think, before you bid me leap the gulph,
To what a fearful depth your victim falls.
Where is the fame, to which I sacrific'd
The feeling idly deem'd beyond temptation?
Can I go forth, and tell the scoffing world
My firm resolves are feeble as their own,

And bear the bitter taunt which waits on him,
Who dares a trial mightier than his strength?

Mir. He, who does well in any rank of life,
May calmly brave the calumnies of men,
And boldly look to Heav'n for his reward.

Aur. Yes, there are duties, public and recluse,
Which to discharge is praise, howe'er we chuse;
But when the choice is made, and bound for ever,
If the recluse return to what he left,
The world will say 'twas appetite alone,
Not his conviction, that produc'd the change,
And hold him an apostate and impostor.

Mir. No more, no more-I see where it must end:-
Aurelio blushes at an act of virtue,
Because some misconstruction waits upon it;
And, therefore, he would have Miranda yield,-
To guilt, which no construction can excuse. [*Exit.*]

Aur. 'Tis well.-Her scorn has giv'n me back myself.-
My pride sustains me now. Aurelio, wake!-
Renounce the hope of those high dignities
Thou may'st aspire to! and for what! A woman!
But such a woman! How! relapsing-Slave!
Bondman to folly and vexation still?-
I will forget Miranda and her charms,-
Nay learn-if possible-to hate her.-Now,
Oh now, poor Agnes, I remember thee. [*Exit.*]

SCENE III.-*The Garden.*

Enter MIRANDA-ZINGARELLA *waiting behind.*

Mir. The monastery must no more supply
A safe indulgence to my chaste affection!
He, whom I fancied rais'd above temptation,
Like the cold ice-alp, which the sun ne'er melts,
Descends to dally with unholy fires,
And tampers with his vow. Farewell, Aurelio!
Yet I must leave my pity with thy fault,
And rate my idle and romantic wish,
That drew thy lonely virtues into peril. [*Exit Miranda.*]

ZINGARELLA *advances.*

Zin. Aye, that's the lady Pedro told me of: and, by the description I have heard of her, she should be Miranda, the long lost sister of Don Christoval. [*Sings.*]

Turn thee, lady, lady sweet!
Listen to me, I entreat!
I've a tender tale to tell-
You will feel-who love so well.

Re-enter MIRANDA.

Mir. Ha! who is this, that seems to know my story?
Approach me, child!-What wouldst thou say to me?

Zin. Pray pardon me, madam-but indeed I must interest you in the saddest story, that ever met your ear-and all who know the lady Miranda are sure that she will listen to the wretched.

Mir. How is it, that thou know'st me for Miranda?

Zin. O, madam, gypsy as I am, I have relations in the church. The gardener of St. Clare's convent is my own brother, and my old father is now endeavouring to procure speech with Aurelio.

Mir. Nay, then, we need not fear an interruption.

What is the story I am wish'd to hear?

Zin. You have heard, madam, of an unhappy nun, named Agnes?

Mir. I have-She perish'd by inhuman rigour.

Zin. So the good Abbot thinks, madam, I am sure. But did he know that she is yet living, and buried by the merciless Domina of the convent, to fall a victim to hunger, and her inexorable revenge, I am certain his pity would relieve the poor sufferer.

Mir. Agnes alive! Doubtless he would relieve her.
For O, he knows how frailty's dusky spots
Stick on the ermine of the whitest virtue. [*Aside.*]
But where is she confin'd?-Say, has your brother
Suspicion of the place of her confinement?

Zin. He does not know for certain, madam. But it is thought, that those, who are condemn'd to expiate any great offences, are usually thrust down into a dungeon in the Cemetery.

Mir. The Cemetery!-As I recollect
It joins the Sepulchre, that appertains
To th' Abbey. Ha! a gleam of light breaks on me!
Retire, good tender girl.-I'll to the Abbot,
And interest him in her swift recovery. [*Exit Zingarella.*]
I did not think to tarry here an hour-
But now there is a cause, which claims me wholly.
Shall not a woman feel a woman's sorrows?
There is a gate, that parts the neighbour graves-
O could I burst its bars, and save this Agnes!-

And why not? Pity's torch burns bright before me,
And lights me to the trial. Mercy lead me! [*Exit.*]

SCENE IV.-AURELIO'*s Cell.*

Enter AURELIO *and Old* ZINGARO.

Old Zin. I knew your reverence would be deeply mov'd
At this poor Nun's distress, and bless the chance
That gave me knowledge she was yet alive.

Aur. No: be assur'd I never meant her penance
Should fasten on her life; and will myself
Demand her from the cruel Agatha.

Old Zin. Thanks, thanks for that.-But I have something more,
Which, while it lays my guilt before your mercy,
Calls louder yet for hearing from Aurelio.
Bet ere I tell my tale I must exact
Your sacred promise of forgiveness, Sir,
For all the injuries which I have done you.

Aur. Injuries done,-and done by thee, poor man!-
But, be this wonder what it may reveal'd,
They cannot be too great for me to pardon.

Old Zin. You may have heard, that they receiv'd you here
An orphan child-Ah! little did they think
That they then buried from his rank and splendor
The long-lost heir of De Medina's house.
Your father was a pillar of the state,
Grave, rigid, just,-let me say unrelenting.-
He persecuted our poor wandering tribe
With such severity, that pity wept.

But he forgot, the meanest may revenge;

And the low worm, that cannot reach the breast,
May strike its deadly venom in the heel.

Aur. Spare these reflections-On!-thy story: briefly!
For, oh! it quickens in my springing soul,
Transports unutterable.

Old Zin. In resentment
I found a way to steal you from his palace;
Baffled all search to find his only son;
And having foster'd with my fittest means
The powers, that open'd in your infancy,
At length I yielded to the gen'ral wish
Of these good fathers, and you took the cowl.
Here I had left you, sunk and unregarded-
Had not the noble spark of merit in you
Flam'd out, and claim'd distinction.-When I heard
From the remotest corner of our country,
The virtues of the excellent Aurelio,
His eloquence divine, his piety,
The miracles wrought by his life and doctrine,
Repentance came upon me. I am ready
With proof to vouch my tale. And now, my fate!-
Whatever you decree, I bend submissive.

Aur. Take my forgiveness!-Take my blessing, father
Of this my better birth. Thou dost not know
How ev'ry word thou'st utter'd glads my heart.
Prepare thy proofs, and meet me on the instant. [*Exit Old Zin.*]
My birth declar'd, absolves me from my vows;

Returns me to the world,-and thee, Miranda.-
O, in one little hour, to be restor'd,
While tottering on the verge of guilt and horror,
To rank, and affluence, and spotless love!-
But, let me pay my gratitude to Heav'n,
Not in the empty sounds of wordy praise,
But in the deeds of mercy. Yes, poor Agnes!
I can now feel a sympathy severe
Impell me tow'rds thee-and I fly to save thee. [*Exit.*]

ACT V.

SCENE I.-*The Grand Square in Madrid.*

Enter CHRISTOVAL, JUAN, *and Soldiers. He marches them round the Stage, and then addresses them.*

Chris. Brother soldiers, I have but a few words to say to you; and to tell the truth, the occasion makes them look so like a speech, that I fear I shall stammer most cruelly. Yet I must explain myself, to benefit by your assistance.

Juan. Tell us but the object, and lead us to achieve it.

Chris. Then it is dearer to a soldier, friends, than even the laurels of his valour-it is a deed of mercy. Brothers, a woman, whose only crime is love, pines in a dungeon; shut with her infant from the freshening day-breeze. She was once, comrades, beauteous as summer, ere superstition bowed her lovely head, and grief wrought winter on it with her tears.-She is dear to me by every tie-Make my cause yours.

Juan. The cause is pity!-We love you, Captain, heartily-To obey you is a duty in all cases.

Chris. Aye, and to feel for woman in distress, is a lesson, which nature wrote upon our hearts, when our first infant cries proclaim'd our wants, and found them answer'd by a mother's love.[1]

Juan. O, no more, good Captain-Lead us to her rescue.

---

1 The exaggerated sentimentality of this scene was typical of late eighteenth-century drama. Whereas *Raymond and Agnes* appeals to the audience's taste for sensationalism, gothicism, and spectacle, Boaden's play embraces the sentimental.

Chris. You speak like an angel-and fight, I know it, like a devil. Pardon me! I was for trying, whether I had not eloquence enough to mould you to my purpose-but a plague of long speeches! The true secret is, to fling your heart upon your lips. One sentence with feeling for its spirit, and virtue for its meaning, sets our nature in a blaze, and all the selfish part of it is blown up in a moment. Now then, my boys, march-and Heav'n bless you! [*Exeunt.*]

SCENE II.-*A part of the Vaults of the Monastery.*

Enter MIRANDA.

Mir. This is the way, as well as I may judge.
The dead, in orderly arranged files,
Leave this uncumber'd path, to tempt me onwards.
O, let me find the intervening gate,
And my strong pity, mightier than my force,
Shall burst its brazen folds, though triple-cas'd.
Spirit of Sympathy! be thou my guide. [*Exit.*]

SCENE III.-*A Sepulchre. A cross, and a lamp burning before it.*

AGNES *discovered, sitting upon the ground, leaning upon a coffin-the lid off, and by her side.*

Agn. How sound he sleeps!-Poor infant, 'tis the same
To him this hideous nursery of horror;
This house of death too,-which, for me design'd,
Serves as a pallet-bed, to shroud his slumbers.
Could I be certain they would save my child,
I'd stretch me, patient, in my last abode,
And thankfully embrace eternal sleep. [*She sinks upon the coffin.*]

[*A noise at the gate.*]

What noise was that?-'Tis not the usual entrance.

Mir. [*without.*] Agnes!

Agn. My name!-and in a voice I know not!

Mir. [*without.*] Heav'n sends you a deliverer! Rise! assist me!
Something secures the gate o' th' inner side.

Agn. Alas! I cannot-My enfeebled joints
Refuse to bear my cumbrous weight again,
And sink me down never to rise.

Mir. O strive-
So near deliverance!-Do but draw this bolt,
Which lies below the lock, and the gate opens.

Mir. So little to perform-and shall I fail?
Can I not drag me on the earth as far,
To bring my child to day-light?-For a moment,
Kind Providence, O string my slacken'd nerves!
One effort!-If I save him, I die happy. [*She attains the door, and draws the bolt-but faints, overpowered by the action.*]

MIRANDA *forces open the gate, and enters.*

Mir. Horrible cruelty!-Thou wretched mother,
Raise thy dejected head: and let the thought
Of promis'd life, and liberty, and love,
Aid thee, to further my weak powers to save thee!

Agn. [*reviving.*] Did I hear truly? Did some friendly voice
Propose to save?-Look there!-O save my child!-
And leave a sorrow-smitten wretch like me,
To bless your charity, and then expire.

Mir. Come, come-Nay, give not all so soon for lost.
Rest yet a little, and we'll venture hence.

Agn. O my preserver!-I had impiously
Parted with confidence and hope together.
I see, no dungeon cruelty can dig,
Male can fill, or innocence inhabit,
Is too profound and strait for dove-eyed mercy
To pierce with succour for the child of grief.

Mir. That power will guide us from this den of horrors!
Let me consider-I must first convey
This tender pris'ner to a kindlier place,
And then return with help to bear you hence.
"She that e'er hopes to live to be a mother,
Feels throbbing in her pure and virgin breast
The sweet solicitude of trembling pity
For helpless infancy"-Heav'n is smiling now,
And fostering, well pleas'd, a deed of mercy. [*Exit Miranda.*]

Agn. Immortal power, preserve my child!-She's gone.
Spirits of peace, O tranquillize my soul,
Or rapture will be deadly like despair.

[*A noise, as of a trap-door heard on the other side.*]

The PRIORESS *is seen coming down with* TERESA.

Ha! they approach-

Prio. Wretched Agnes,
Whom all the mercy I intended marks
But deeper with the brands of guilt and shame,-
Answer me, how hast thou divulg'd a secret,
Which I thought never could have pass'd these walls?

Agn. No:-I will never implicate by weakness
One whose rash pity risk'd ev'n life to save me.

Prio. Trifle not with my vengeance, wanton-Know,
In spite of all thy arts, it comes to crush thee.
Thou art to die-and this thy hour appointed.

Agn. Ha! I'm lost!-

Prio. You have disgrac'd your order and your convent,
Publish'd your infamy, and our dishonour;
Therefore you die.-Behold! the means are ready.

Agn. Poison!-What, shall I aid my own perdition?

Prio. Take it-Be brief.

Agn. For your eternal welfare,
Let me but live on hour for preparation!

Prio. What! till the partner of your crime shall come
With sacrilege to snatch you from my grasp?
I know the whole of your complotted guilt.
No: now this moment!-Nay then! [*Offers to strike.*]

AURELIO *rushes in through the gate, followed by* HILARIO *and* BONAVENTURE.

Aur. Hold your hand!
Is this the way that leads to penitence?
These vaults of death, are they holy means
By which the feeble are restor'd to goodness?
Merciless! horrible! Religion thus
Loses its sacred character and office;
Converts to bigot rage, and rends the heart
Its all-forgiving Author bids to heal.

Agn. Thus-in the dust, I bless the pitying hand,
Which bruis'd me in its justice but to save me.

[*A shout without.*]

CHRISTOVAL, RAYMOND, LORENZO, JUAN, *and Soldiers break in.*

Ray. My life, my Agnes!-we will part no more. [*Agnes faints.*]

Lor. O, my dear sister!

Aur. Bear hence those vile women.
[*Another shout without.*]

[*Exeunt* PRIORESS, TERESA, HILARIO, *and* BONAVENTURE.]

Chris. Haste, reverend Aurelio, to the Convent!
The people furiously assail the walls,
And nothing but your presence can restrain them.

Aur. Be ready to resist them, if I fail!
Though there is virtue in their sympathy,
Yet violence is not the march of justice.
Where there are laws, the laws alone should punish. [*Exeunt* Aurelio, Juan, *and Soldiers.*]

Ray. Lift up thy head, my Agnes-See, thy brother.
But ah, I tremble to enquire-our child-

Enter MIRANDA.

Agn. He lives-is safe.

Ray. May I believe it true?

Mir. Yes, I preserv'd him-Nay, no thanks to me.

Whate'er my future lot, thus to have sav'd
One innocent, is transport to my soul-
A joy too bright for misery to cloud.

Agn. Where is the other saviour of my life,
Who snatch'd me from the dagger's point-Aurelio?

Mir. Did he? Aurelio!-Blessings, blessings on him!

Chris. And now, Lady Runaway, if you have done with your prayers, vouchsafe a word to Captain Christoval:-for, though a Nunnery is the last place I thought of finding you in, I believe you are my hopeful sister, Miranda.

Mir. Brother, you're not deceiv'd-'tis she herself;
Who, wild and visionary as she seems,
Feels for her Christoval the truest fondness.

Enter AURELIO, ZINGARO, ZINGARELLA, ANTONIA, *&c.*

Aur. Miranda here!-Thou mistress of my fate!
Why, I have news to tell thee, my Miranda,
More strange than all the miracles before us.
The secret of my noble birth reveal'd,
Confirm'd by proofs too evident for doubt,
Dispenses me from the monastic state;
And might I hope you would accept my hand,-

Mir. Away reserve, and maidenly resentment!
To be permitted to receive his vows,
Whose sympathising goodness has preserv'd
Repentant Agnes to a happier life,-
Thus virtuous, thus to call thee mine, Aurelio,
Is bliss unutterable!-

Chris. Is this the end
Of all your wanderings, my gentle sister?

Ray. My Agnes, let me lead thee from this place.
Trust me, thy sufferings well shall be aton'd.

Aur. As heir to De Medina, all the pow'r
That I have lies at your disposal, Sir.

Zin. Now, now, Antonia, is your time to speak.

Ant. One wonder yet remains-You said Medina-
If you are he, I kneel before my brother.

Aur. My happiness is more than I can bear.
Please you, retire within the Abbey-walls,
And so repose awhile. Events like these
Fever the mind with its own best emotions.
Miranda, come, my love, my monitress!-[1]
With safety may I give me to the world,
While you direct me-my unerring guide!
Our passions are the fairest gifts of Heav'n!
Their just indulgence is our proper joy:
'Tis their perversion only makes us wretched.[2]

THE END.

1 *monitress*: in other words, Aurelio views Miranda as a woman who will monitor and correct his behavior. This attitude is typical of the late eighteenth-century and reflects the belief that women were endowed with more virtue and sensibility than men.

2 Perhaps an allusion to the passions run amok in *The Monk*.

AIRS, GLEES, AND CHORUSSES
IN A NEW
GRAND BALLET PANTOMIME OF ACTION,
CALLED
RAYMOND AND AGNES;
OR, THE
CASTLE OF LINDENBERGH

Airs, Glees, and Chorusses
In a new
Grand Ballet Pantomime of Action,
Called
Raymond and Agnes;
Or, the
Castle of Lindenbergh

Composed by Mr. Farley

Now performing at the Theatre-Royal Covent-Garden

London:
Printed by T. Woodfall, No. 104, Drury-Lane,
For T.N. Longman, Paternoster-Row. 1797.
[Price 6d.]

In order to shape the Episode of *Raymond* and *Agnes*, from the romance of the Monk, for dramatic effect, the situation in which the Countess (step-mother of Agnes) is placed in the cottage, according to the romance, is now occupied by AGNES. Another variation occurs in making the NUN, whose SPECTRE appears, the *mother* of *Agnes*, and former Countess of Lindenbergh.

The progress of the story will occur in the following fences.

BALLET

Raymond and Agnes;
Or the
Castle of Lindenbergh.

SCENE I. *A Gothic library in the castle of Don Felix.* - Raymond discovered as this studies, is interrupted by the entrance of Don Felix (his father) who informs him it is his wish he should go upon his travels. – Theodore, his favourite domestic, intreats to accompany him. – After which the scene changes to

The outside of a castle. – Theodore takes an affectionate leave of his favorite (Annette). – Several servants enter, preceding Don Felix, Raymond, and a holy father of the Church-Raymond receives their benedictions, and departs on his journey, accompanied by Theodore.

Scene. *Madrid; with a view of an hotel and a convent.* – PROCESSION of NUNS and FRIARS – Chorus. (See page 11) Agnes, the daughter of Count Lindenbergh's departure from the convent – Raymond and Theodore enter, order refreshments from the hotel, and proceed on their journey, under the guidance of Claude, one of a banditti infesting the neighboring forest.

Scene, *A forest – midnight, with a defiant hovel.* – Enter Baptiste (one of the banditti) disguised as a woodman – The carriage with Raymond and Theodore breaks down – Claude, pointing to the hovel, informs them they may there find shelter for the night.

Scene, *A nearer view of the hovel.* – Baptiste is seen to enter it. – Raymond and Theodore are conducted in by Claude and Baptiste.

Scene, *Inside of the hovel.* – Maugerette and her child are discovered. Raymond and Theodore are introduced by Baptiste – Theodore is shewn to his room by Maugerette – Robert and Jacques (sons to Baptiste) enter armed, making a servile obedience to Raymond, who is conducted to his chamber by Robert.

Scene, *The bed room prepared for Raymond* – Maugerette wishing to preserve the life of Raymond from the assassins, conveys a pillow stained with blood upon his bed, thereby to inform him of his danger – she conceals herself – Raymond retires to rest, but is prevented by finding the bloody pillow and struck with horror, falls into a swoon – Robert enters – Attempts to murder him – Is prevented by Maugerette – and Raymond, at her request, retires.

Scene, *The Lower Apartments of the Hovel.* – Robert informs his father and brother of the ineffectual attempt on the life of Raymon; who is brought in by Maugerette – A knocking is heard without – Agnes (who has been also benighted in the forest) is led in by Claude, attended servants – Supper is prepared – Opiates mixed with the wine – Agnes drinks, and falls into a slumber – Maugerette begs Raymond not to drink, but to put on the semblance of sleep – Baptist fends Robert and Jaques to secure the servants, who have retired; and supposing Raymond at rest, prepares to murder him – Raymond seizes him, and Baptist falls by the hand of Maugerette – who points out a secret avenue; through which she, taking her child, Raymond and Agnes escape, followed by Theodore.

Scene, *Inside of Lindenbergh Castle.* – The mother of Agnes, the late Countess, pourtrayed in the habit of a Nun. – The Count discovered viewing the picture with agitation – kneels to implore forgiveness for the murder. – Agnes brought in by Raymond, is introduced to the present Countess – she becomes enamoured of him, offers him her picture, which he rejects with scorn.

Scene, *The Chamber of Agnes* – Portrait of a Nun, with a wound upon her breast, a lamp, dagger, and a rosary on her arm. – Agnes enamoured of Raymond, enters, and prepares to draw his Portrait – Raymond entering unperceived, throws himself at her feet, and obtains a promise of her hand – He requests an explanation of the picture of the bleeding Nun. – She informs (in a Song), see page 12, 'tis the resemblance of a Spectre which haunts the Castle every fifth year. – The Count and Countess approach; and in anger order Raymond to quit the castle.

Scene, *The Outside of the Castle* – Raymond, about to depart, is diverted by the sound of Mandoline – a paper is lowered by Agnes from the Castle, containing a drawing of the Nun, with the following scrolls.

"When the castle-bell tolls one,
"Expect me like this bleeding Nun."

Scene, *The outside of the castle as before* – Raymond waiting for the appointed time – the clock strikes one – the gates fly open – the apparition of the nun comes from the castle – Raymond (supposing it Agnes) follows in extacy – Theodore approaching, is met by Agnes in the habit of the nun – agitated by the apparent neglect of Raymond, they retire.

Scene, *A dreary wood* – Raymond following the spectre (still supposing it Agnes) attempts to embrace it when suddenly vanishing, a cloud rises from the earth bearing the following inscription :–

"PROTECT the CHILD of the MURDER'D AGNES."

Scene, *The Mountains* – Robert, Jacques, and Cluade (the Robbers) discovered at the grave of Baptiste – Theodore and Agnes enter – Agnes is seized and borne into the Cavern.

Scene, *A wood* – Theodore and Maugerette meet Raymond and inform him of Agnes being seized by the Robbers – They hasten to her rescue.

Scene, *Inside of the Cavern* – The three Robbers cast lots for the possession of Agnes – she becomes the prize of Robert – He attempts to sieze her – She resisting, he aims a stiletto at her breast. – At this instant Raymond, Theodore, and Maugerette rush in – Robert falls by the Dagger of Raymond, Jacques by the sword of Theodore – and Claude by a pistol from the hand of Maugerette.

Scene, *The castle of Don Felix.* – Raymond presents Agnes to his Father, who joins their hands; and the piece concludes with

A FINALE SPANISH FANDANGO

CHARACTERS of the BALLET.

Don Raymond – *Mr. Farley.*
Don Felix – *Mr. Hawtin.*
Count Lindenbergh – *Mr. Cranfield.*
Theodore – *Mr. Simmonds.*
Baptiste – three Robbers – *Mr. Delpini.*
Robert – three Robbers – *Mr. Follet.*
Jaques – three Robbers – *Mr. Blurton.*
Claude (a postilion,) like-wife a Robber of the gang – *Mr. Simpson.*
Countess of Lindenbergh *Mrs. Follet.*
Agness (her niece) – *Mrs. Mountain*
Annette – *Miss Burnet.*
Maugerette *Madam. De la Croix.*

The vocal part by
Messrs. *Grey, Linton, Street.*
Mrs. Henley, Mrs. Castelle, Miss Leserve

Airs, Glees, and Chorusses
In Raymond and Agnes

Chorus.

Some yield their breath to hoary time
And others perish in their prime
But he whom death the longest spares,
Is but the witness of most cares

Air – Agnes

Full fifteen years have past away
Since first within these walls,
Appeared the ghost, whose gliding form

The stoutest heart appals.
Long time here nightly stalk'd this bleeding Nun,
Her entrance at the awful hour of one!

II.

Her face she'd veil, and on her arm
A chaplet still appear'd
One hand a burning lamp sustain'd,
A dagger t'other rear'd;
O what amazement to behold the Nun,
When ent'ring as the midnight clock struck one!

III.

At chamber doors she'd sometimes stop,
And heave a piteous wail:
Now curses deep wou'd shake the rood,
Now anthems soft prevail.
At length the spectre for a time seem'd gone
And ceas'd her visits as the clock struck one!

IV.

Now each fifth year, on May's fifth morn,
Still constant to the hour;
That door she passes and descends,
The steps of yonder tower:
And then that Gothic hall she'll cross anon,
Just as the warning midnight bell strikes one!

AIR – Agnes.

When warn'd this Castle to depart,
On me fond glances Raymond threw;
Love seiz'd for once a Parthean dart,
And gave him victory as he flew.

GLEE – Muleteers.

Bring, bring the generous stalk to cheer,
The weary, dropping Muleteer!
Those Alps, whose tops in clouds are lost,
Since break of morn with toil we crost,
O full of danger is the way!
The Wolf twice mark'd us for his prey;
With sudden swell the torrent broke;
The winds with loudest fury spoke!

O bring the generous flask to cheer
The spirits of the Muleteer!
Bring too the Flagelot and Tabor,
To soothe the heart, and sweeten labor,
The dance, the dullest mind will brighten,
The foot most weary it will lighten!
Lara, lara, lol,
Lara, lara, lol!

Such joy the ev'ning yet can give:
The day till twelve at night will last,
And when in merriment 'tis past,
We've only one day less to live!
Your smiles, ye Damsel, too shall cheer
The spirits of the Muleteer!
Lara, lara, lol,
Lara, lara, lol!

FINALE.

STRIKE the lute's enchanting wires!
Every chord the dance inspires!
In the brisk *Fandango* meeting,
And with smiles each other greeting;
The *Castinet* shall time our measure,
And the night dissolve in pleasure!

FINIS.

Suggested Reading List

The Monk Matthew G. Lewis

"The Castle Spectre" Matthew G. Lewis

The Italian Ann Radcliffe

Mysteries of Udolpho Ann Radcliffe

The Castle of Otranto Horace Walpole

Gothic Readings: The First wave, 1764 - 1840 Edited by Rictor Norton

"Life of Kemble" James Boaden

"Life of Mr. Siddons" James Boaden

Dracula Bram Stoker

Frankenstein Mary Shelley

www.ingramcontent.com/pod-product-compliance
Lightning Source LLC
Chambersburg PA
CBHW021930040426
42448CB00008B/990

9781943115013